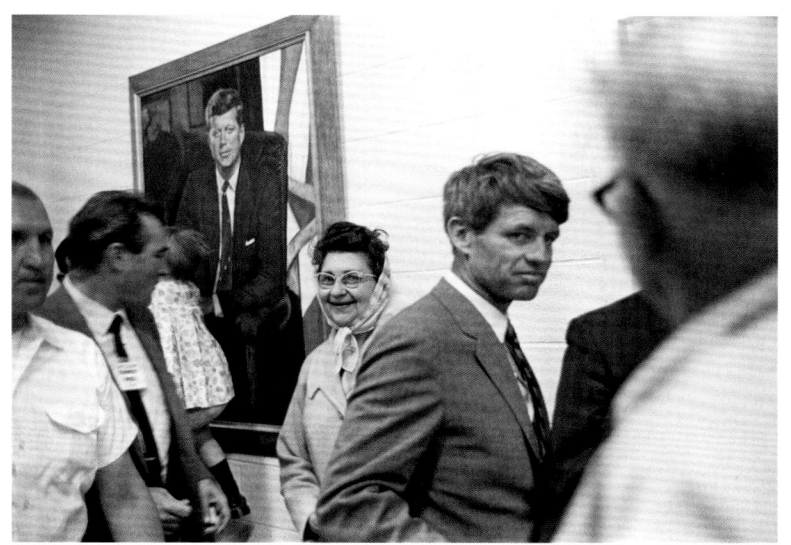

"The most important thing is anticipation. Not where the action is taking place, but where it's going to take place. Not where the subject is now, but where they're going to be."

LAWRENCE SCHILLER

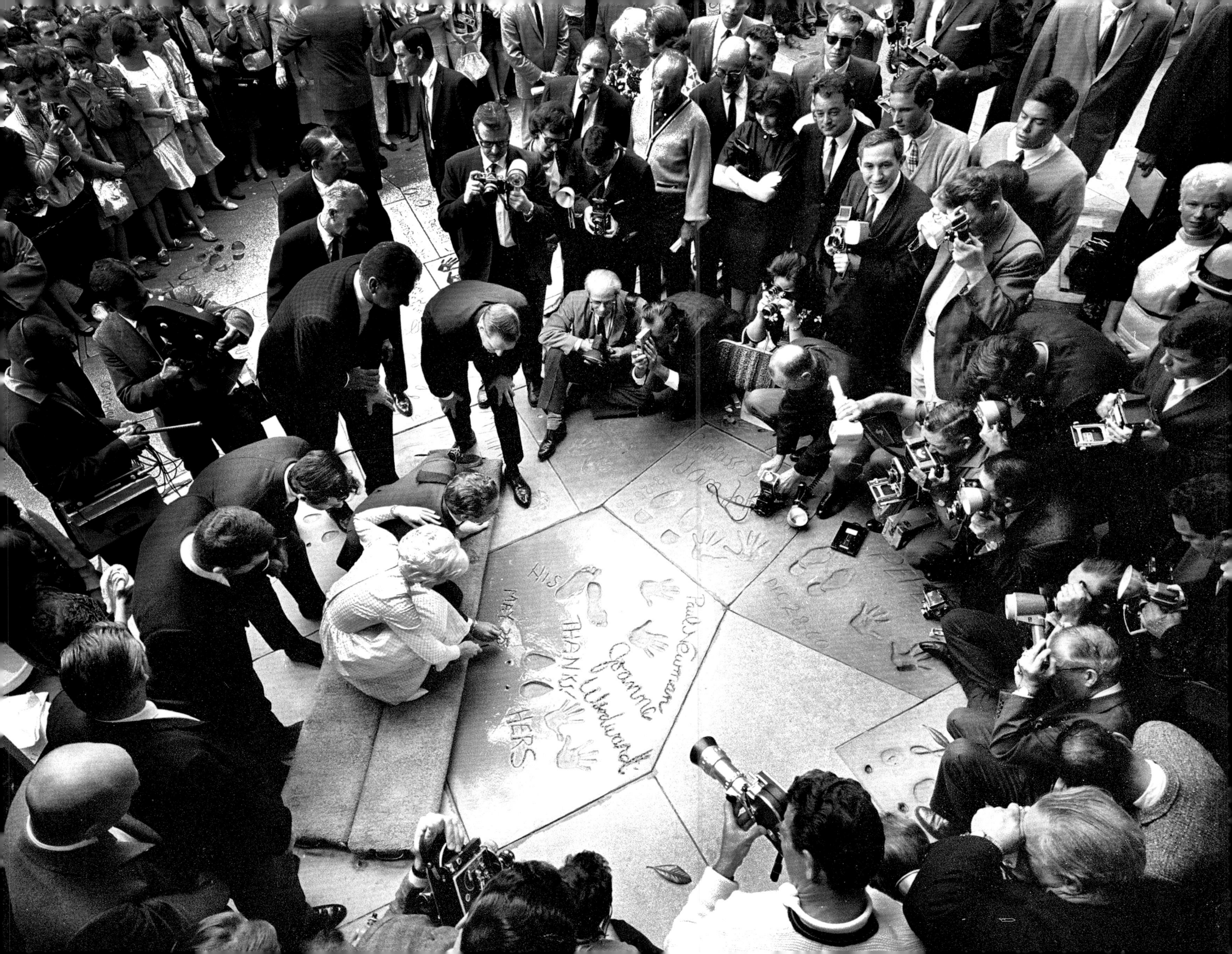

LAWRENCE SCHILLER

PHOTOGRAPHS

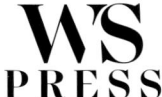

WS
PRESS

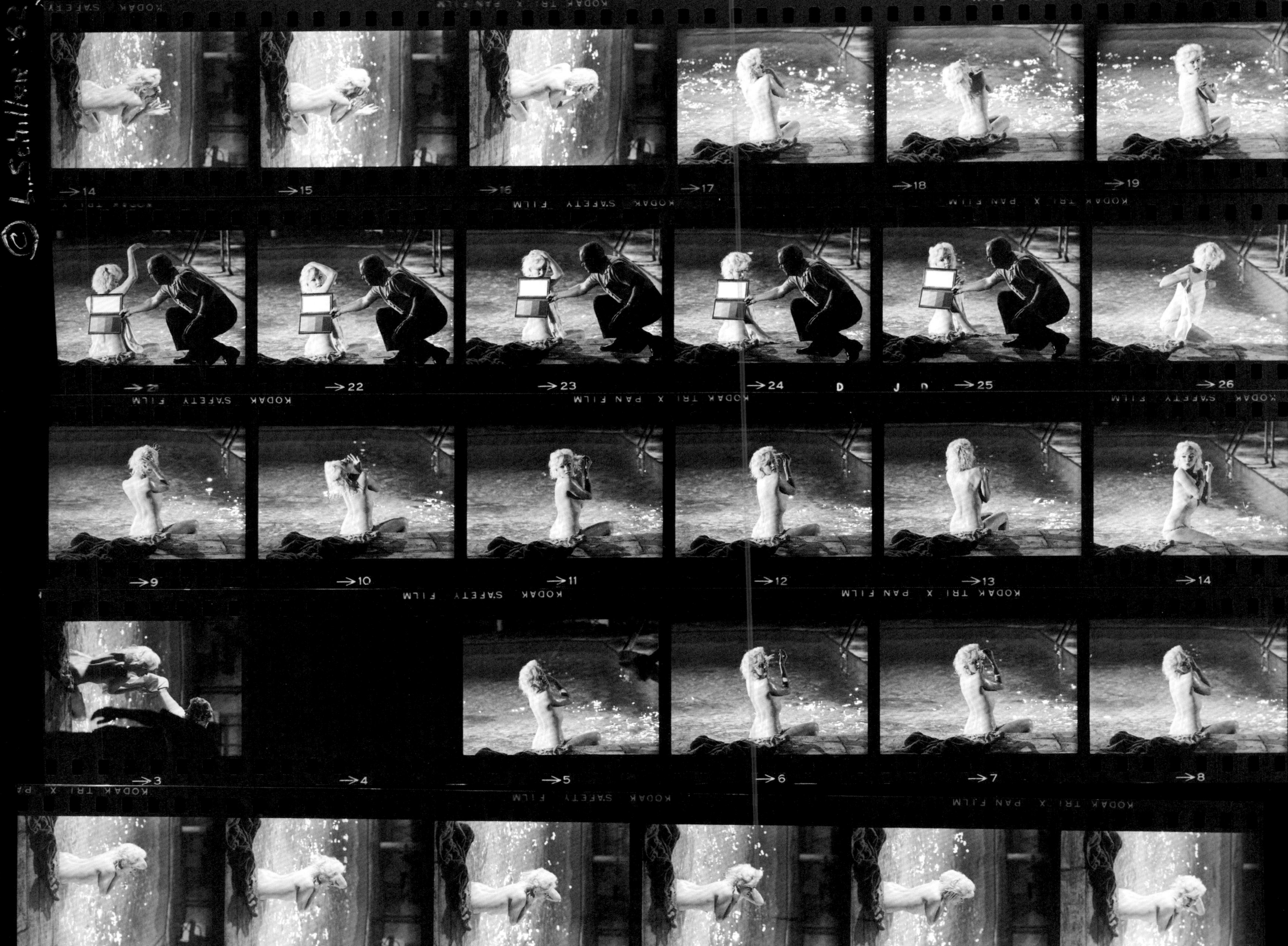

I first used photography as a way to see the world. My father gave me a camera, an East German Exakta, for my bar mitzvah, and I carried it with me everywhere I went. By the time I was sixteen, I had already won several major photography awards and traveled across the country to cover sporting events. As far as I was concerned, it was more exciting than school.

The first time I visited the Time-Life Building in New York City, I was seventeen. I found myself in the elevator looking up at the legendary (and very tall) photographer Margaret Bourke-White. When I asked her for some advice, she replied, "Just remember to make sure you're alive when you die."

Despite my young age, *Paris Match*, *Life*, *Look*, *Stern*, *Newsweek*, *Time*, the *Sunday Times* (London), and the *Saturday Evening Post* — the biggest publications in Europe and the U.S. — soon had enough confidence in my ability as a photographer to trust me with big assignments. So, one month I was working for *Sport* magazine and the next for *Life*. And a lot of the time it wasn't the editors calling me, but me pitching them. The advantage I had by working as a freelancer was that no one editor could pigeonhole or typecast me — so I wasn't just a sports photographer or a news photographer or a celebrity photographer.

At the start of the turbulent and tumultuous Sixties, I was only twenty-three, but I had been a professional photographer for about a third of my life. It was the dawn of the "Golden Age of Photojournalism," and everything was moving past my camera awfully fast. I think of that decade as being like the Wild West, an uncontrolled period. Whenever a headline-making news event occurred, I was there. By the end of the Sixties, I had covered so many stories, my photographs were becoming part of American history.

When the 1960 presidential election results came in and Richard Nixon lost, I captured the tears of his wife, Pat Nixon. When Marilyn Monroe agreed to pose for her first nudes since reaching stardom, I photographed her for *Paris Match*. When Buster Keaton made his last appearance on a motion picture set, there I was, photographing him for *Life*.

When Lee Harvey Oswald was apprehended after the assassination of JFK and interrogated at the Dallas Police Headquarters on November 22, 1963, I was covering it for the *Saturday Evening Post*. When the Watts riots erupted in 1965, a picture I took wound up on the cover of *Newsweek*. When Muhammad Ali knocked out Floyd Patterson, my photos appeared in *Sport* magazine. When my multiple-exposure nude of dancer Paula Kelly appeared in the August 1969 issue of *Playboy*, it was the first time the post office allowed a photo showing pubic hair to be sent via the U.S. mail, expanding the boundaries of men's magazines.

And when Twentieth Century-Fox hired me to photograph Paul Newman and Robert Redford during the filming of *Butch Cassidy and the Sundance Kid*, I suggested the addition of a still montage in the film and wound up directing it. Not long after that movie was released, I was in New York with Dick Pollard, the picture editor of *Life*. With a television in almost every home now, he told me, all the magazines I was working for would soon be out of business. "You're young enough to walk across the street," Pollard said, "from one corner to another."

Every once in a while, you come across someone who sees something in you that you yourself don't understand. For me, that person was Paul Newman when he gave me the chance to direct. Before I knew it, I was working for Paramount Pictures, which got me into my first jobs directing motion pictures. I knew it was time to put my cameras away, follow Pollard's suggestion, and walk across the street to a new corner.

MARILYN MONROE

"You're already famous, now you're going to make me famous,"
I said to Marilyn as we discussed the photos I was about to
take of her on the set of *Something's Got to Give.* "Don't be so
cocky," Marilyn replied, "photographers can be easily replaced."
Nothing could have prepared me for the day Marilyn jumped
into the swimming pool in her bathing suit and eventually came
out with nothing on.

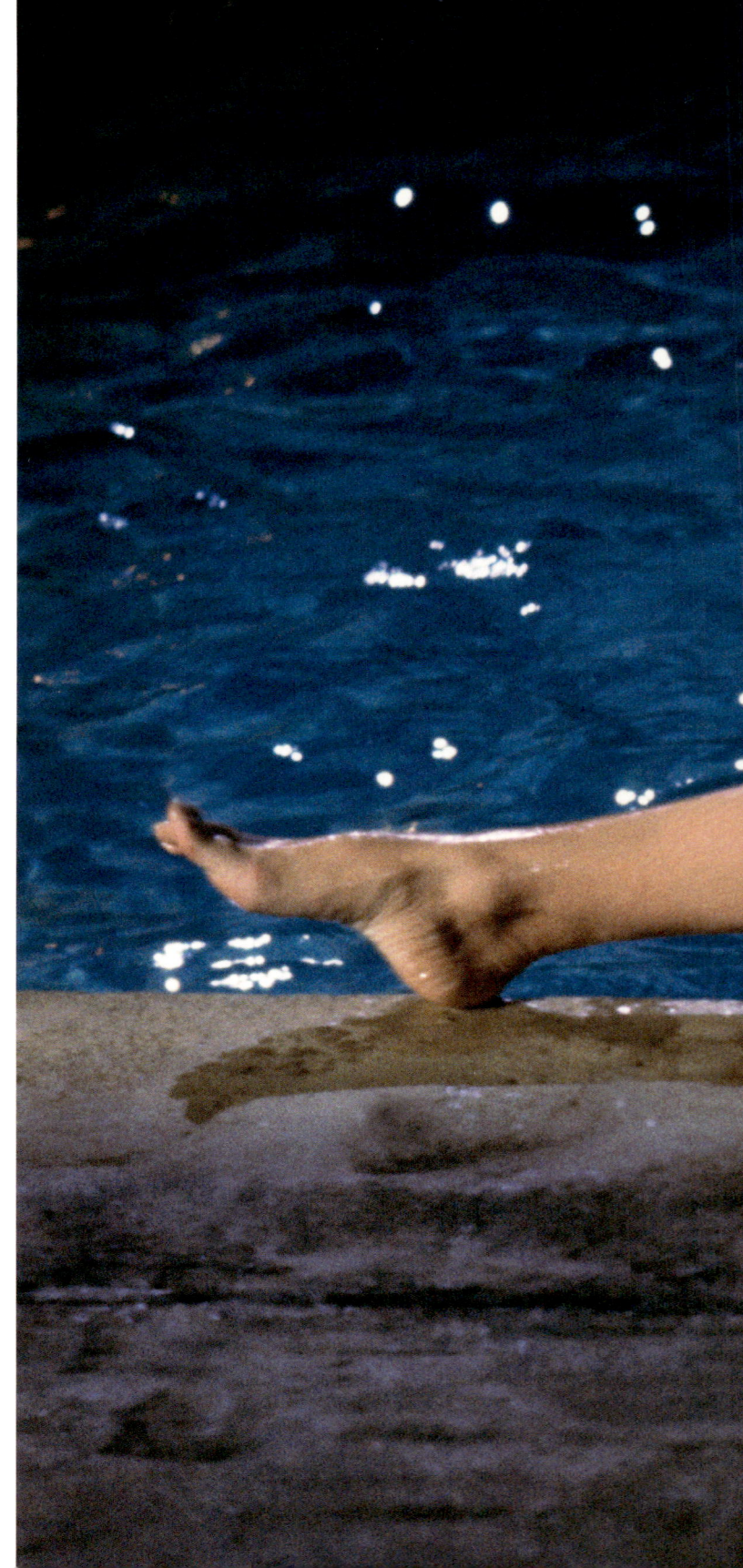

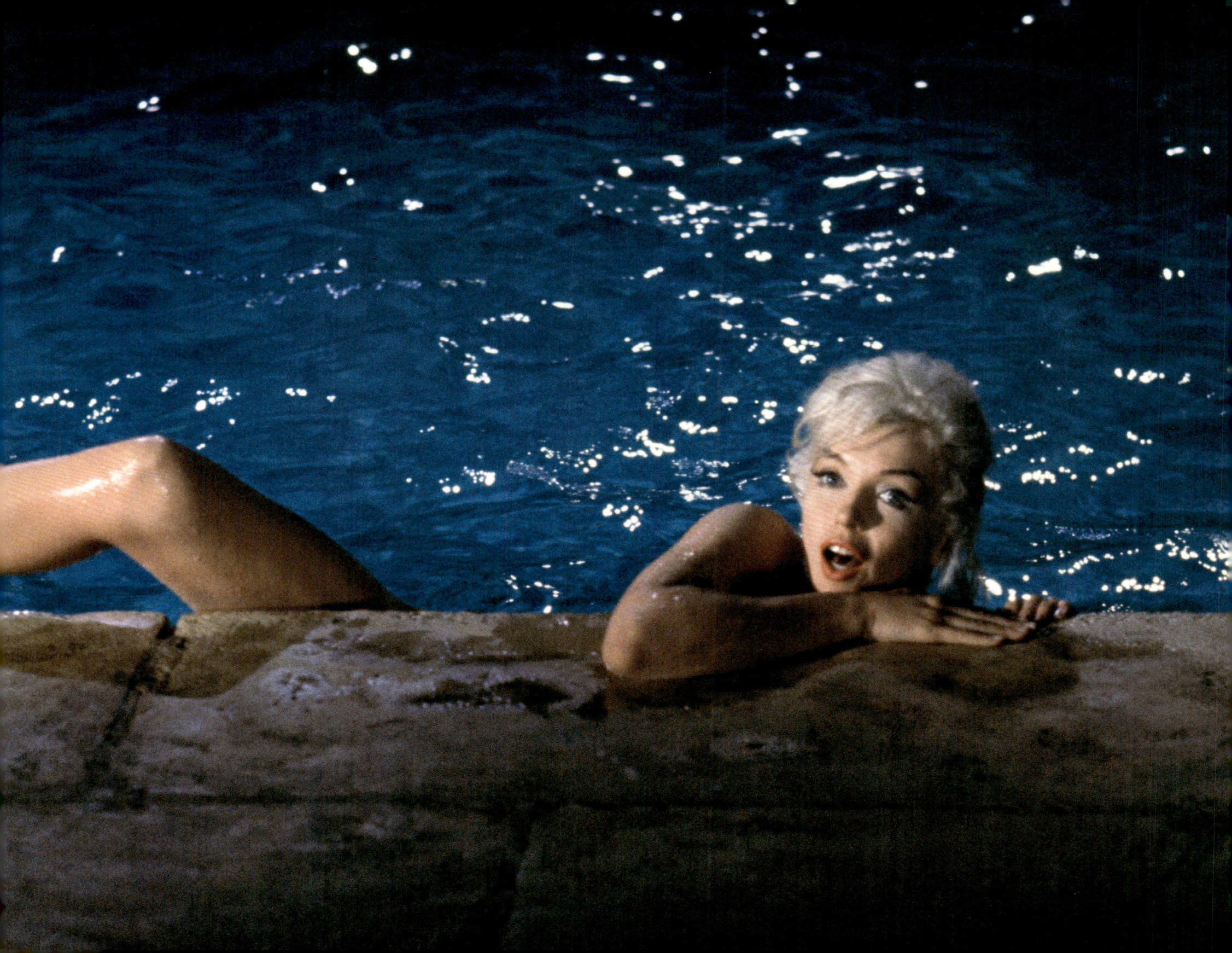

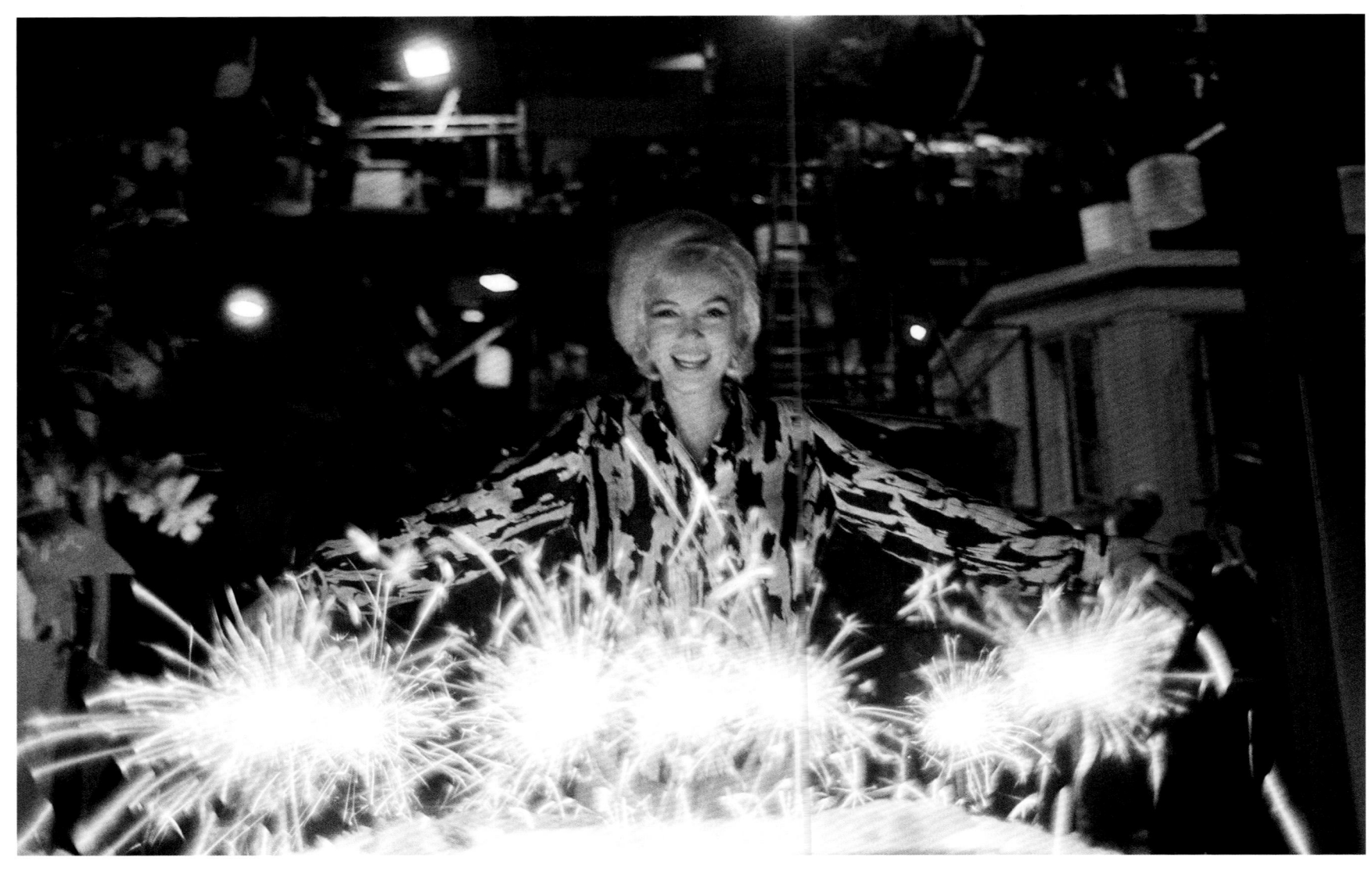

Friday, June 1, 1962, was Marilyn's thirty-sixth birthday. Late in the day, the cast and crew came together to celebrate with her. A huge birthday cake was brought in, with sparklers for candles, and Marilyn posed behind it looking joyful and appreciative. It was unimaginable that two months later she would be dead.

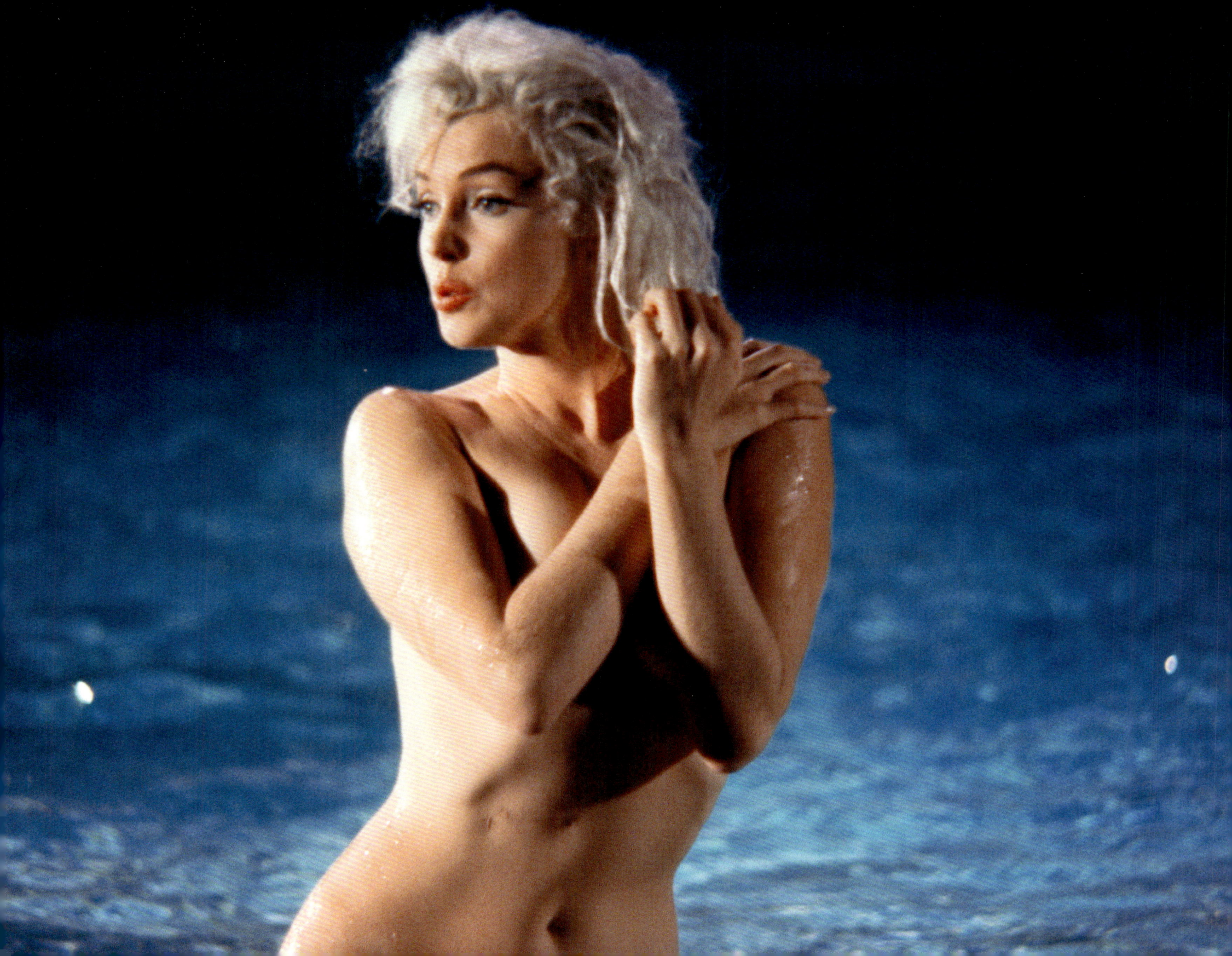

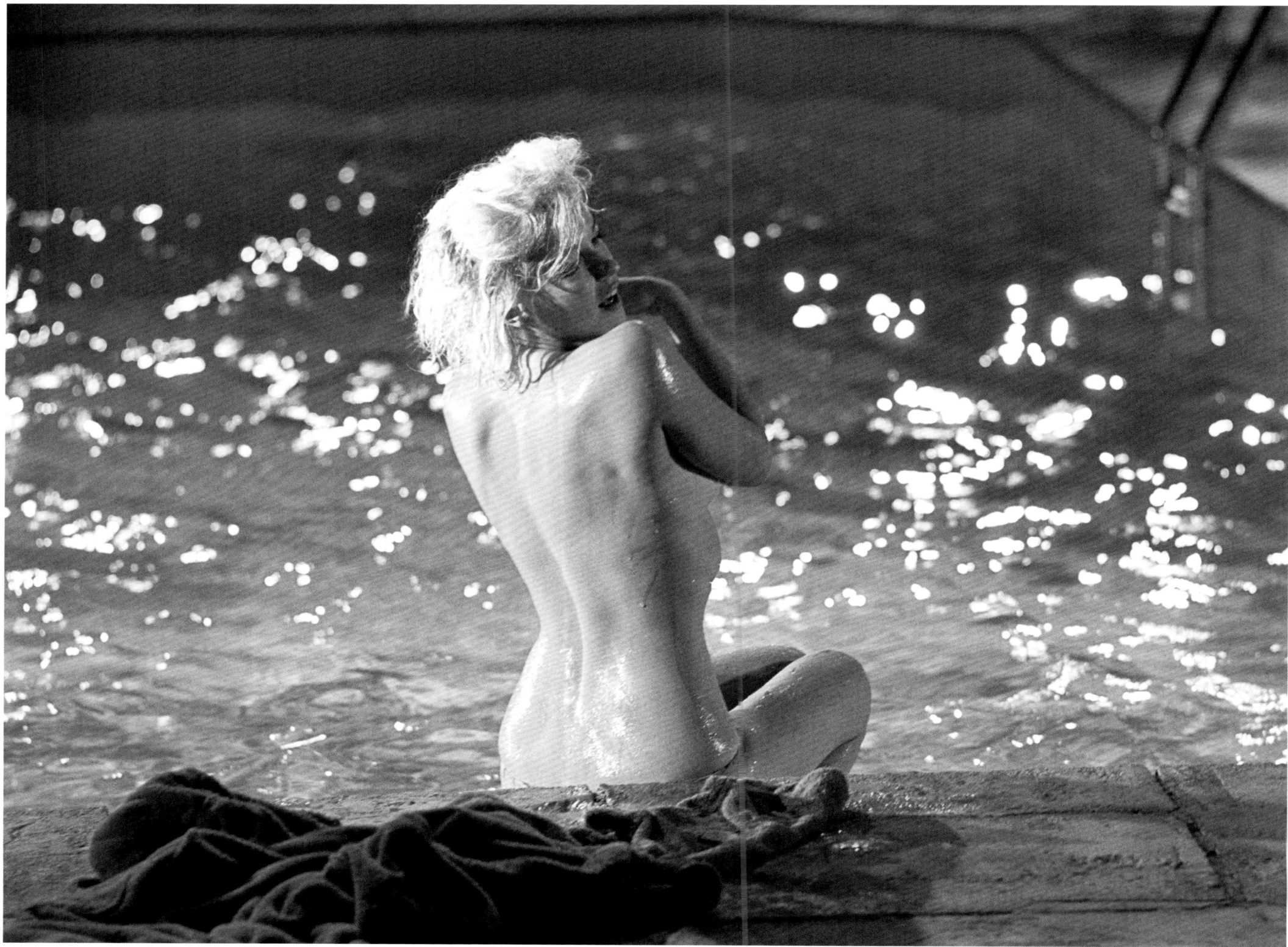

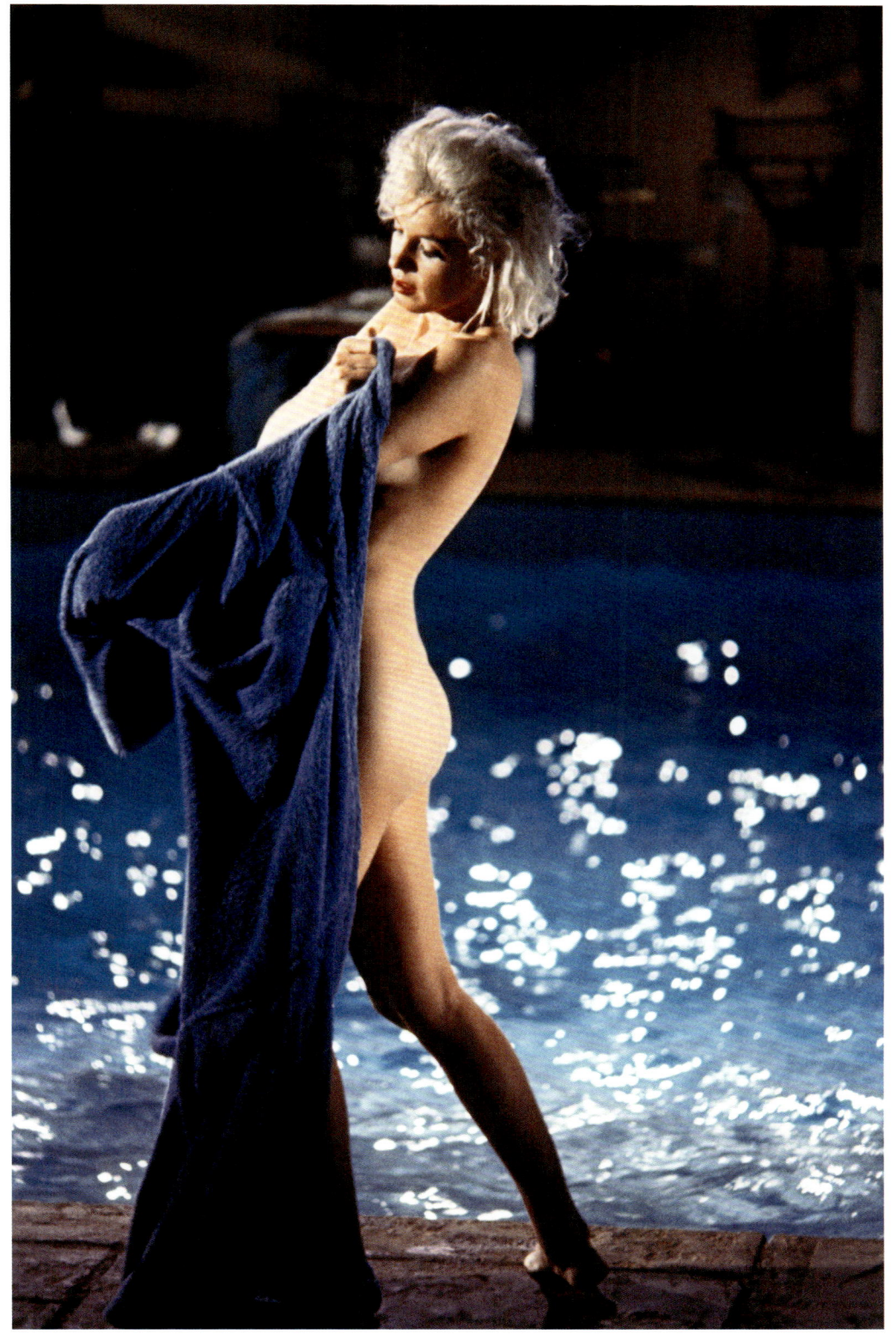

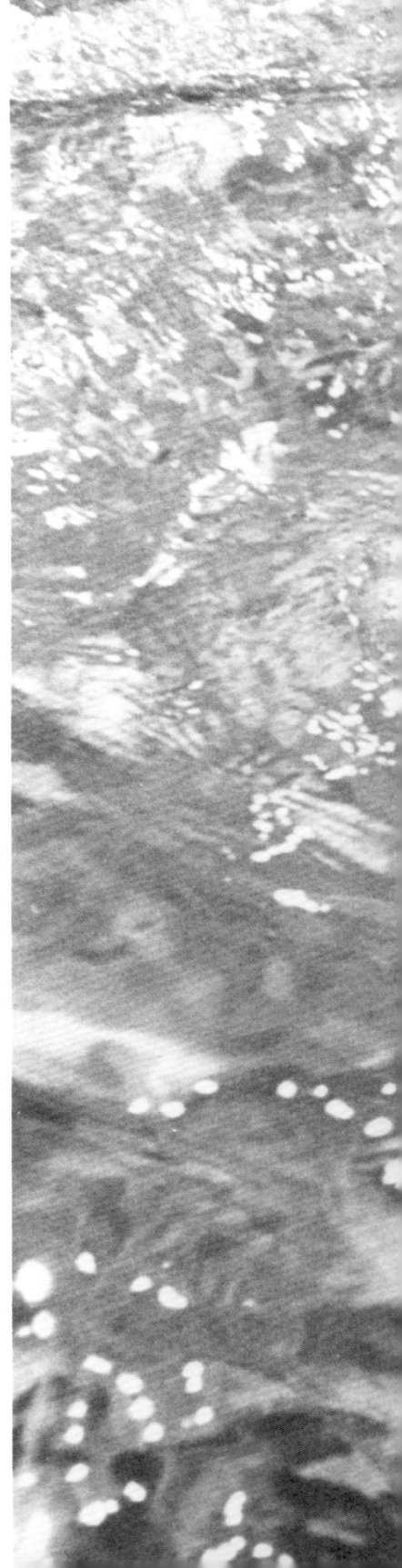

Marilyn was a photographer's dream subject with her clothes on and even more stunning with them off. While naturally insecure and shy, when the cameras rolled, she came alive. There was no hint of the woman who had been in trouble for most of her life. Her wet skin glistened. Her smile was provocative. She looked as good as she had ever looked. As I shot, I was sure that the pictures I was taking were going to be unforgettable.

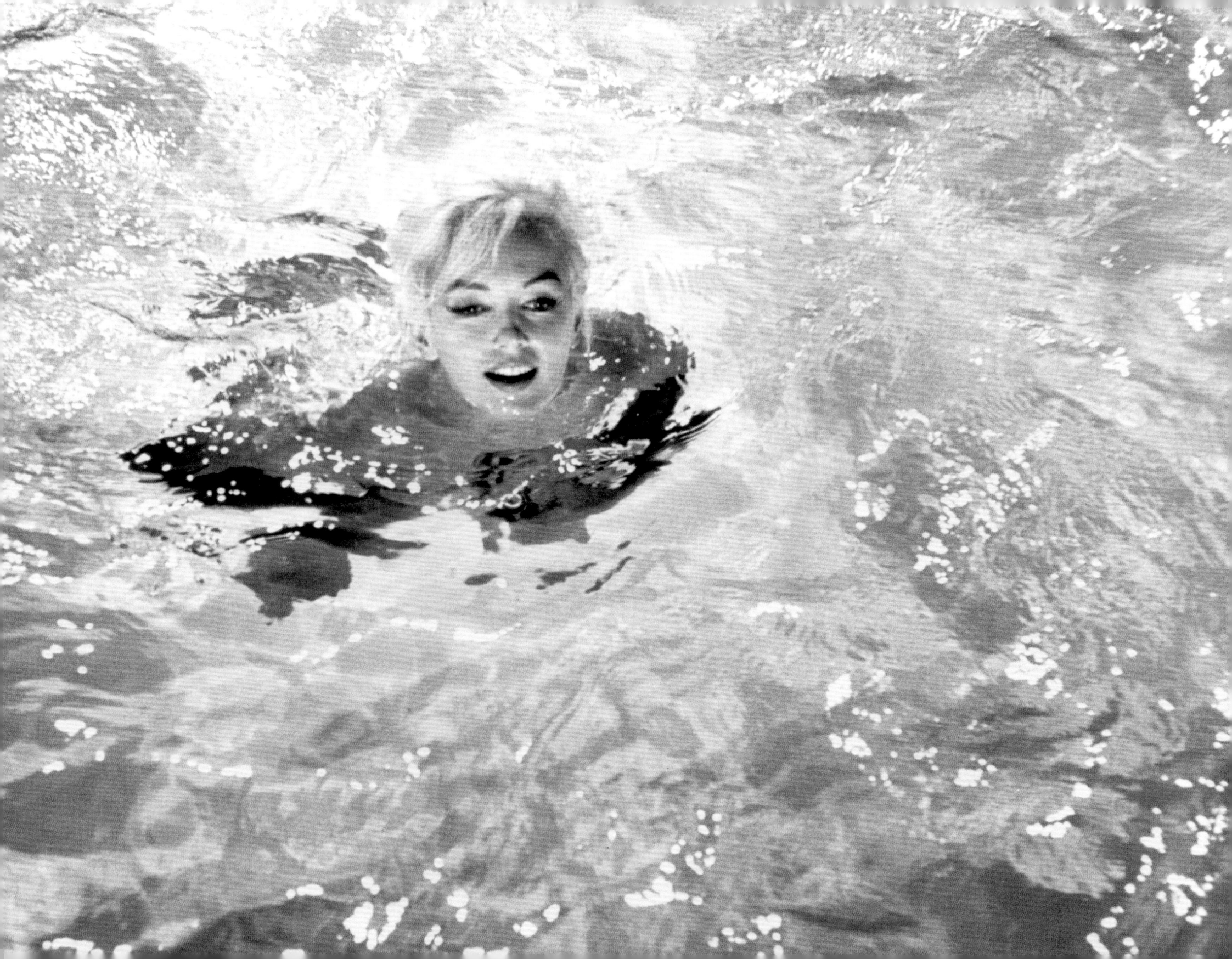

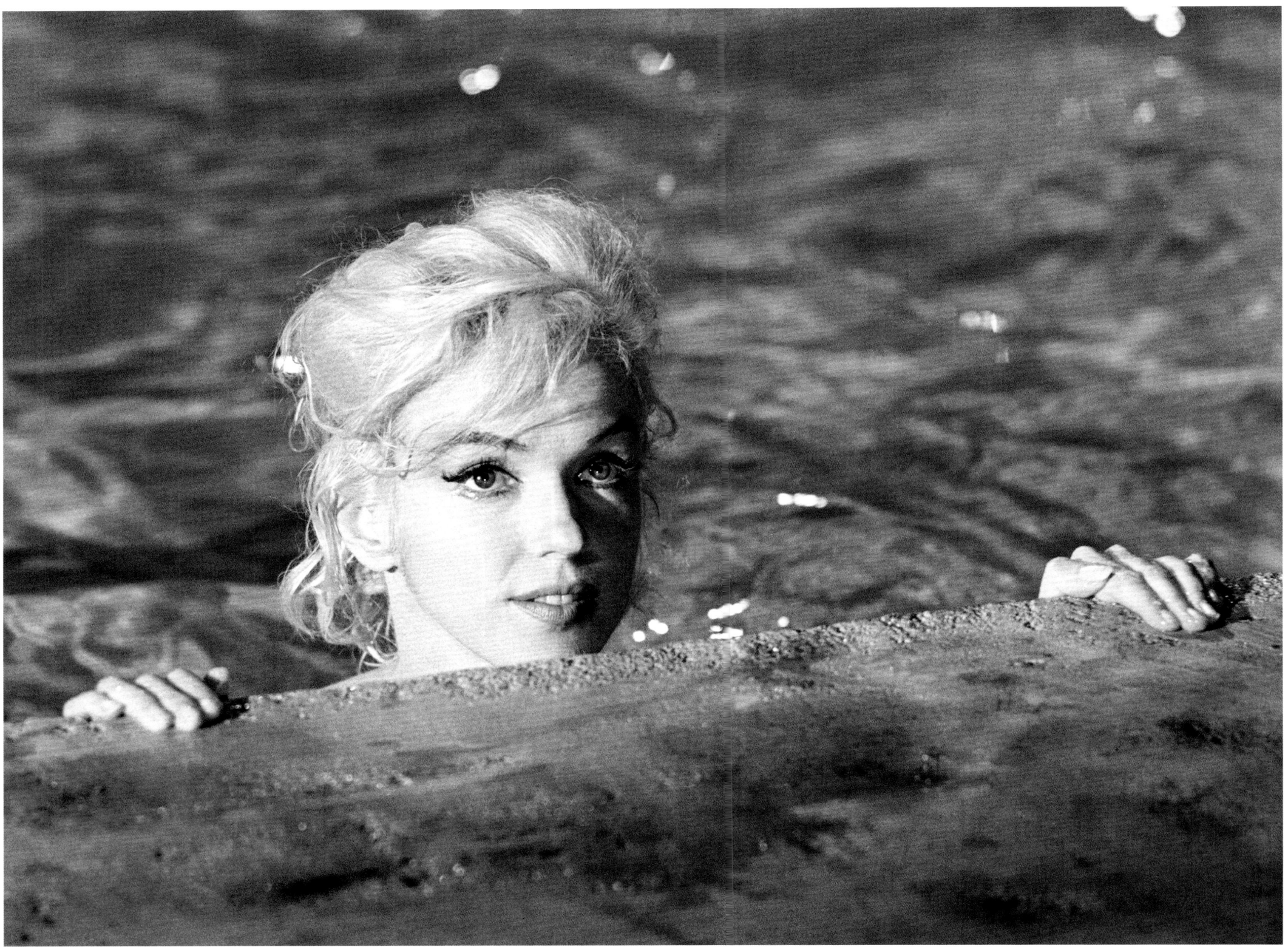

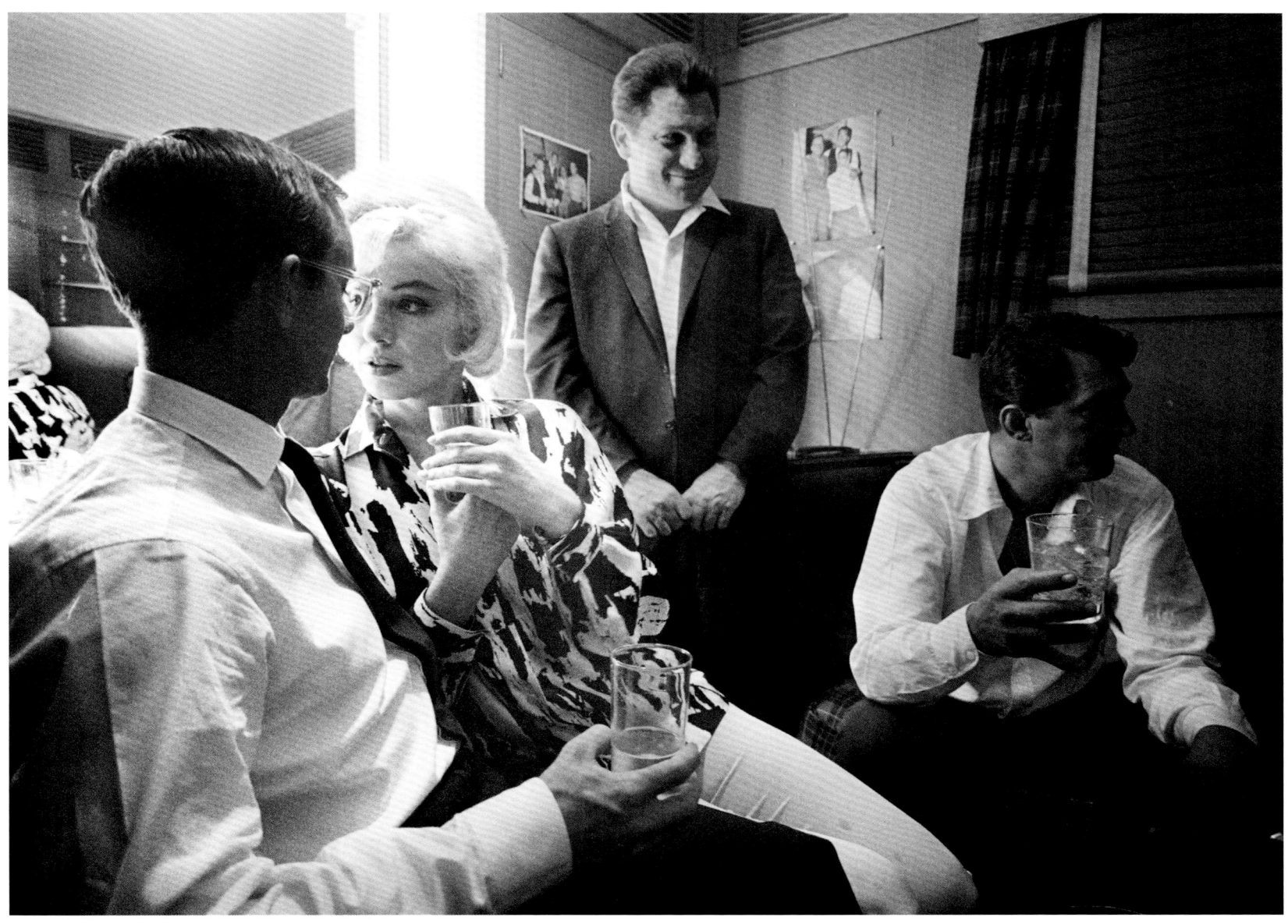

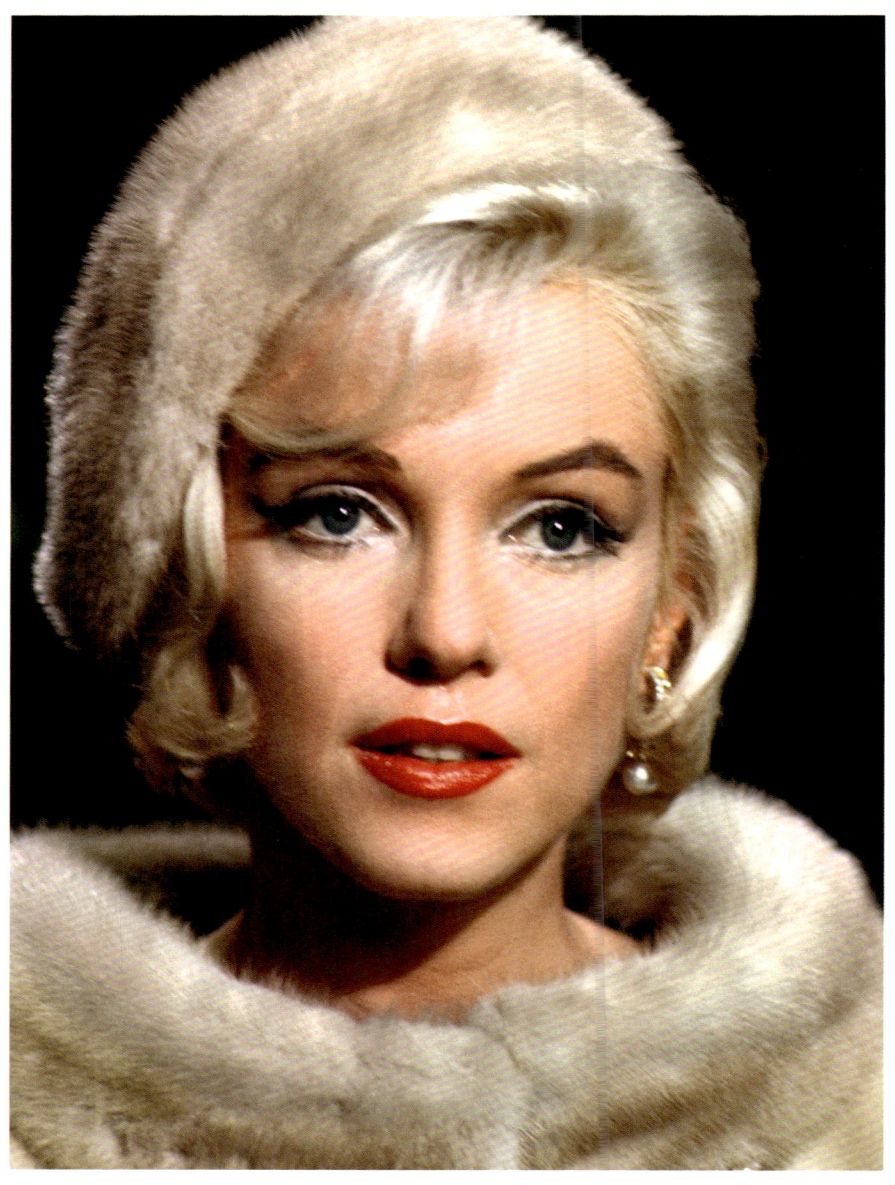

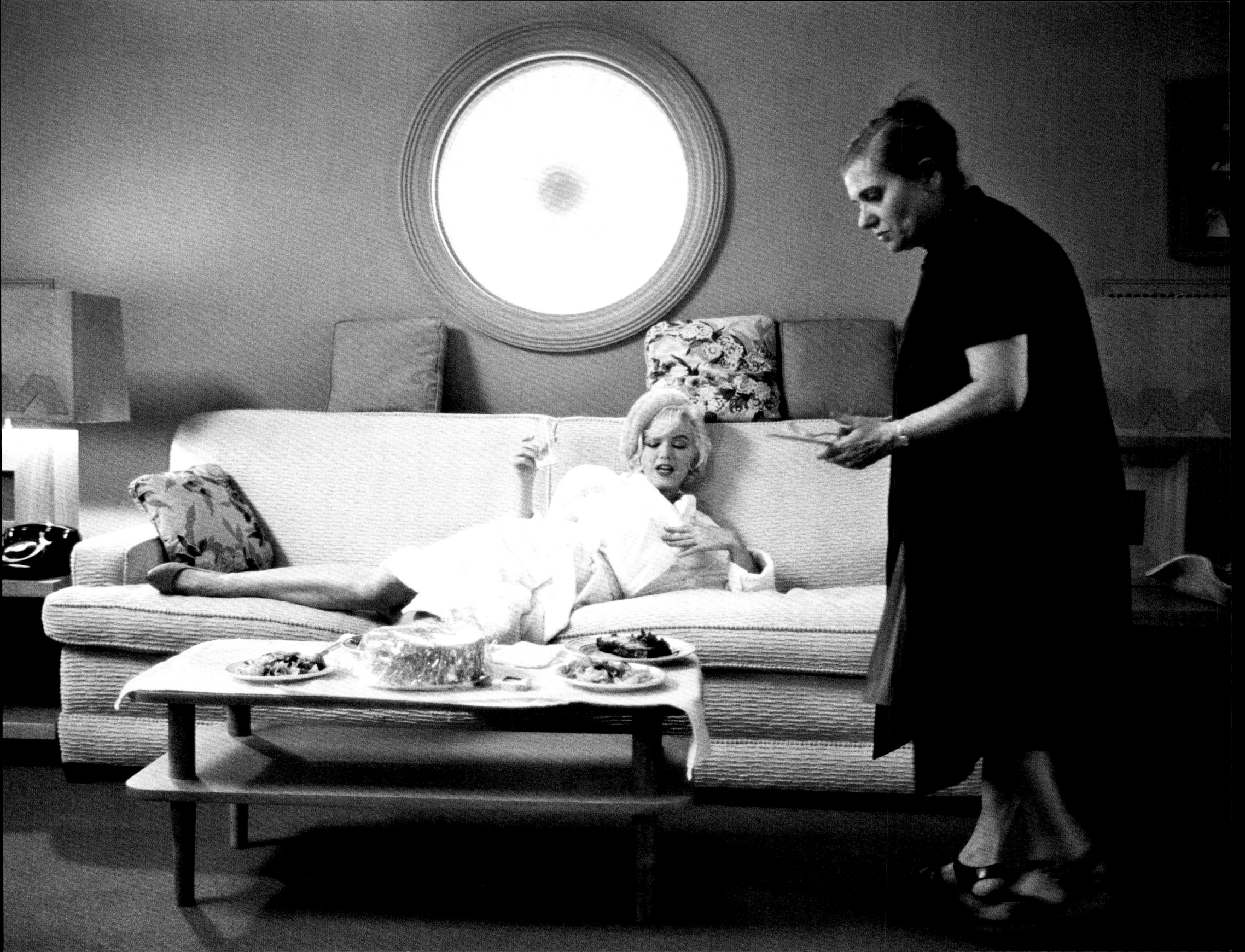

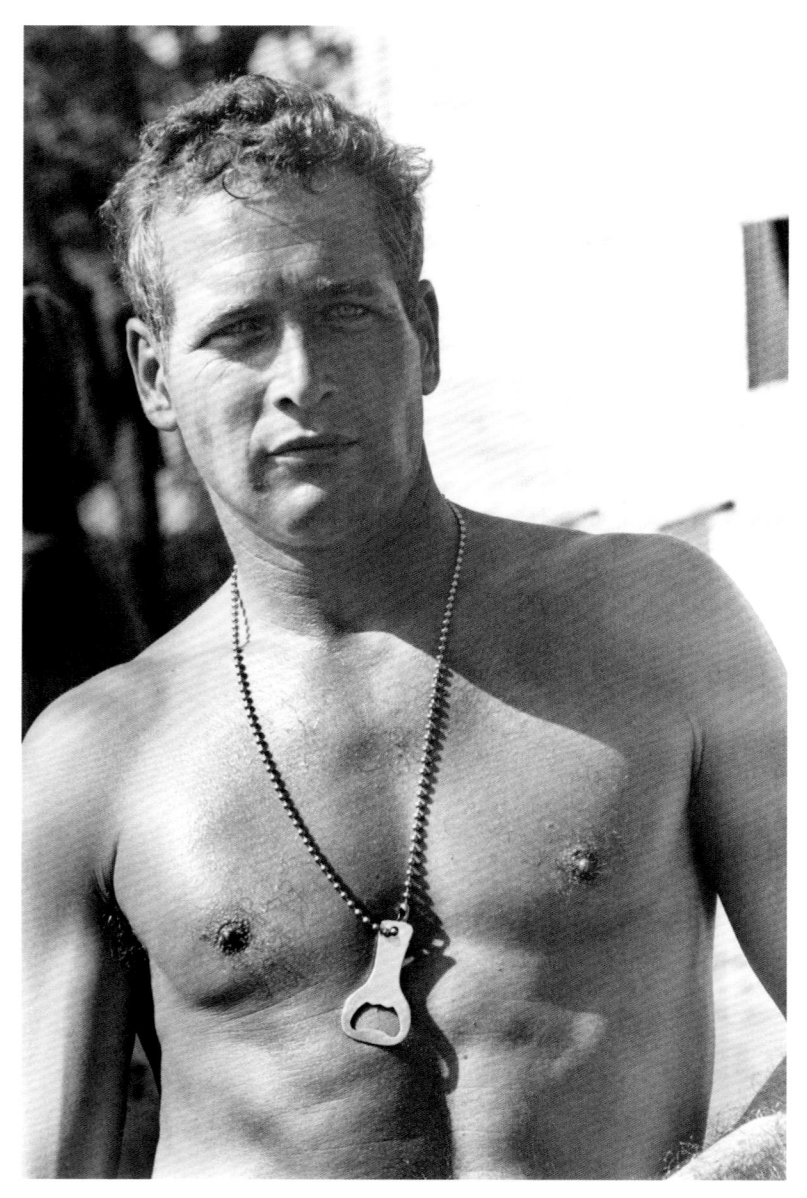

N E W M A N
+
R E D F O R D

I photographed Paul Newman on four films in the 1960s. During the shooting of *Cool Hand Luke*, he was always drinking beer during the day and sweating it out in a portable sauna at night. On the set of *Butch Cassidy and the Sundance Kid* in Mexico, he and Robert Redford would play ping-pong between camera setups. Newman was the more competitive one; he drove race cars and loved to win. Redford was more sensitive; he later founded the Sundance Institute and encouraged young filmmakers throughout the world.

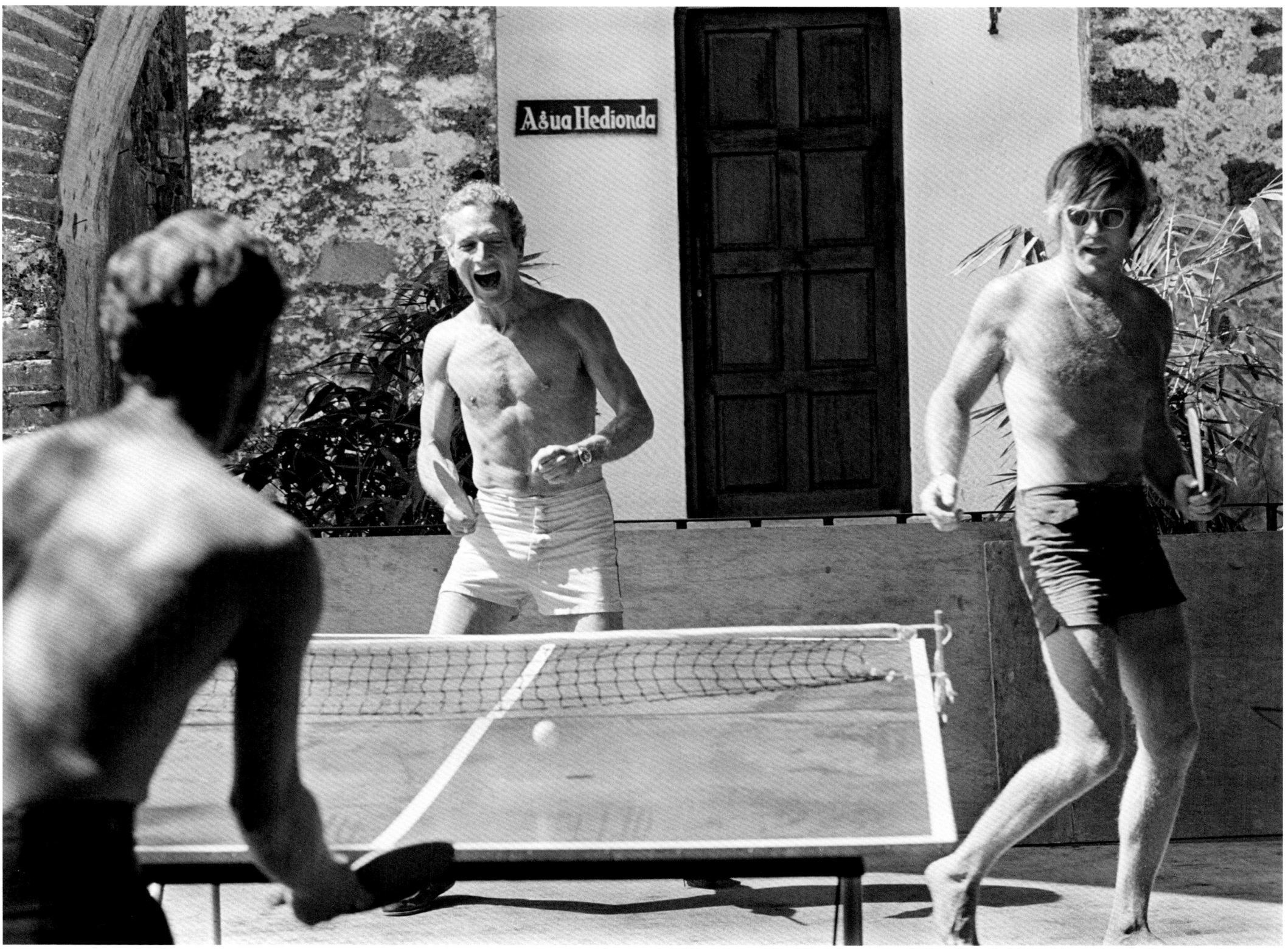

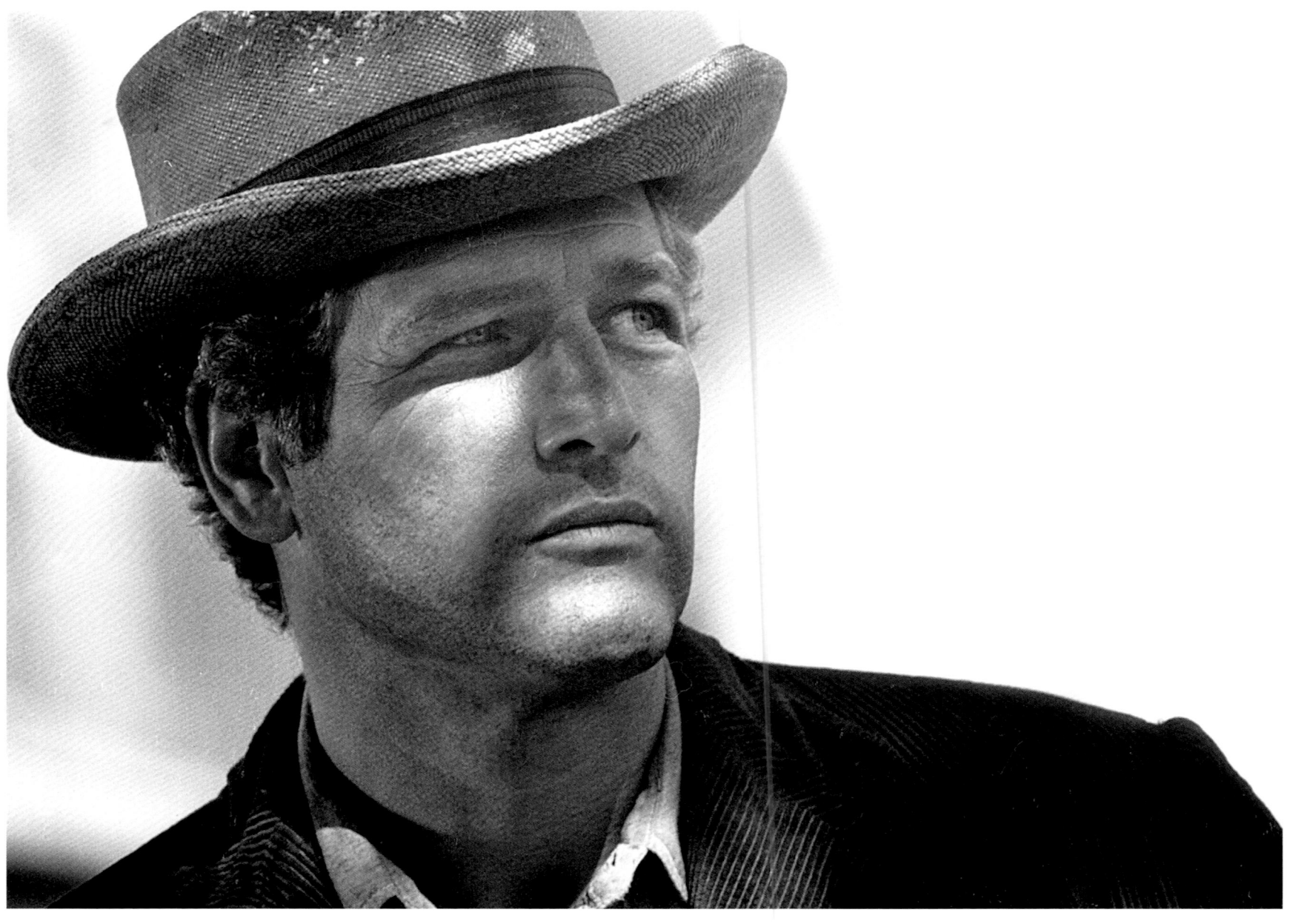

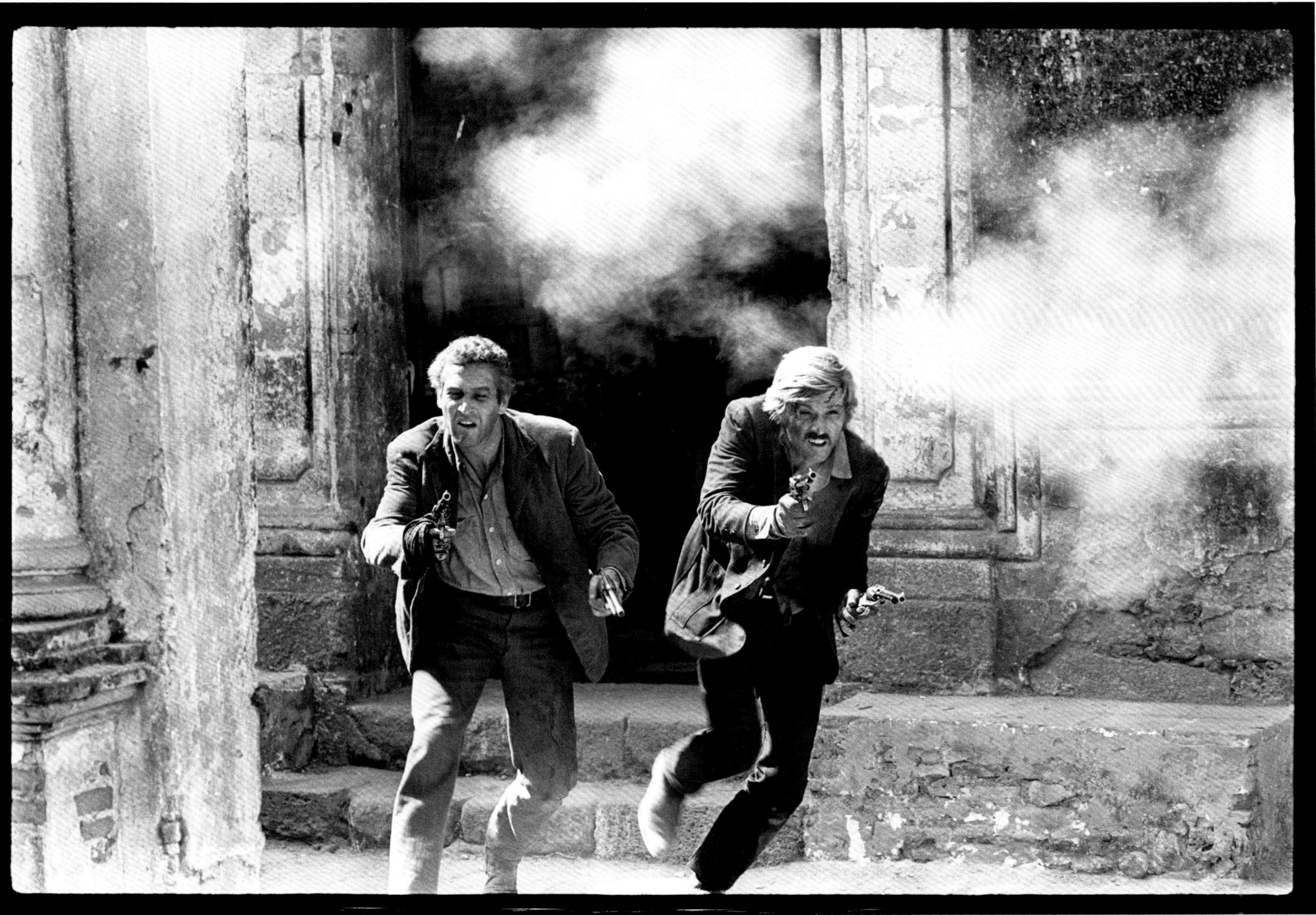

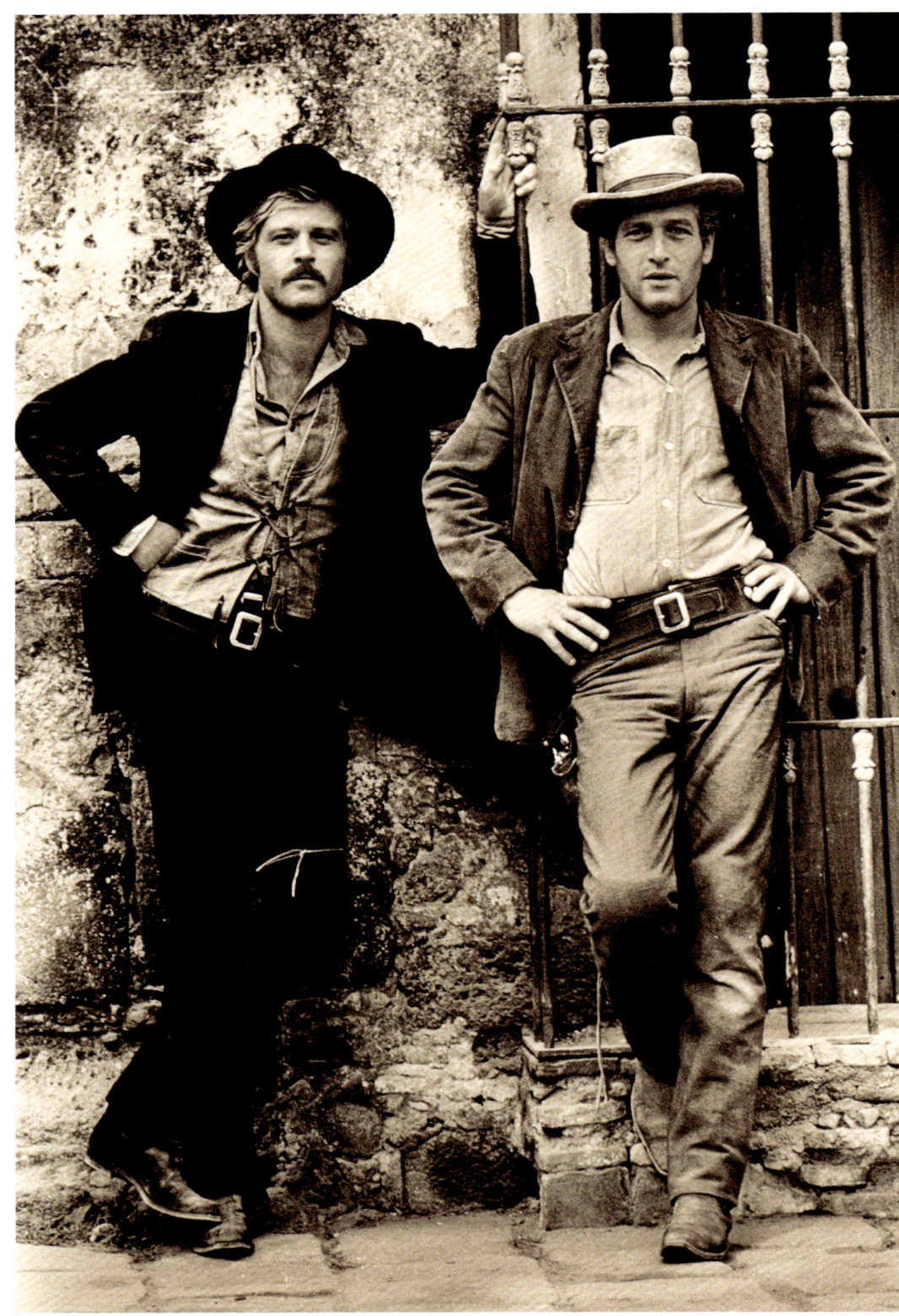

By 1968, Newman was at the peak of his power as America's leading man. He was *Butch Cassidy*'s producer as well as its star, and he created one of the most memorable duos in the history of film when he hired little-known Robert Redford to co-star. In full costume, gun belts strapped around their waists, boots unpolished, shirts unwashed, they were defiant, untouchable, sure of themselves.

Butch Cassidy won four Academy Awards, and remains one of my favorite films of all time. Pure entertainment. Even the most serious moments in William Goldman's script are done with humor, wit, and irony. Paul Newman opened a new door for me by giving me the chance to direct five minutes at the heart of the film.

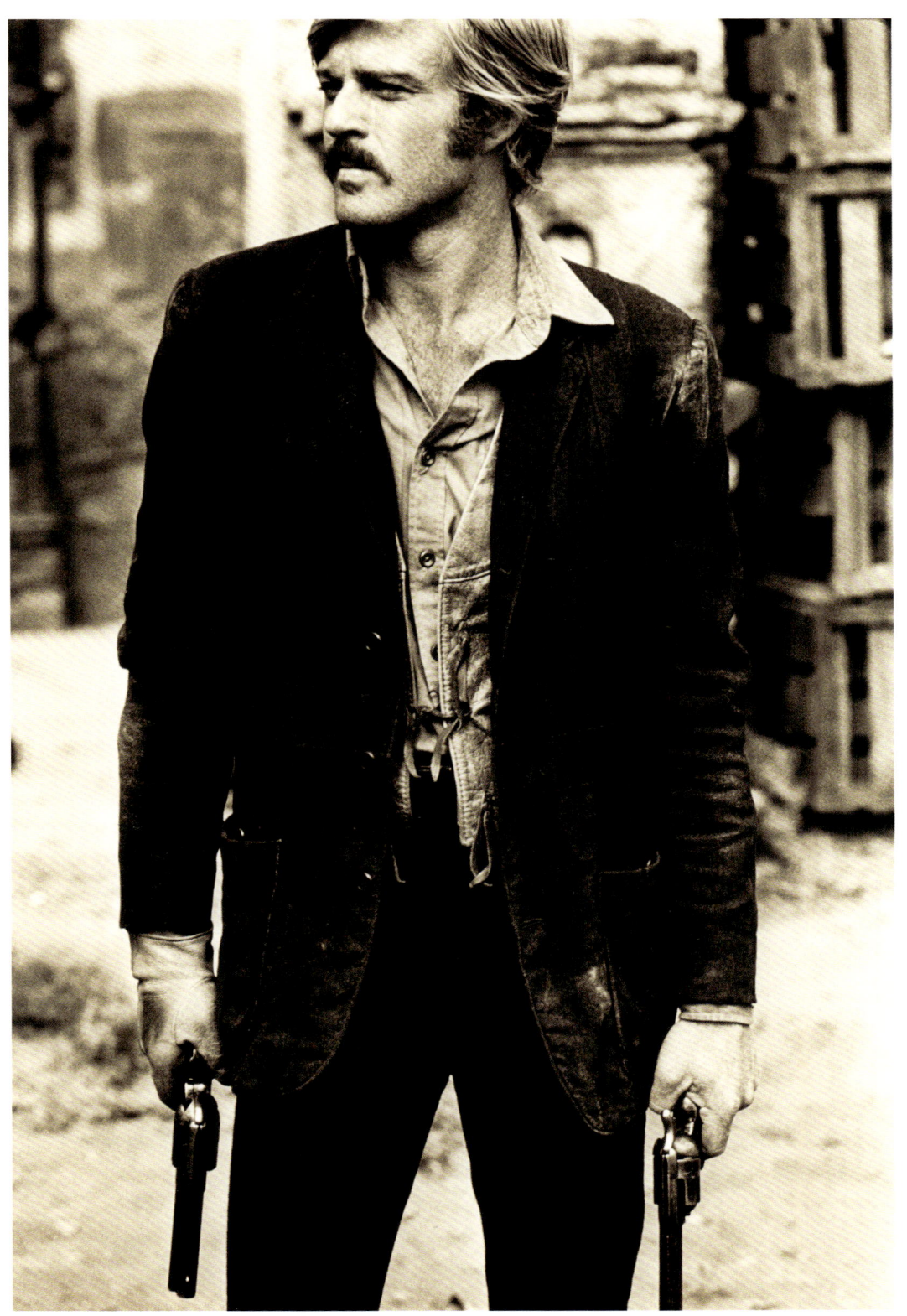

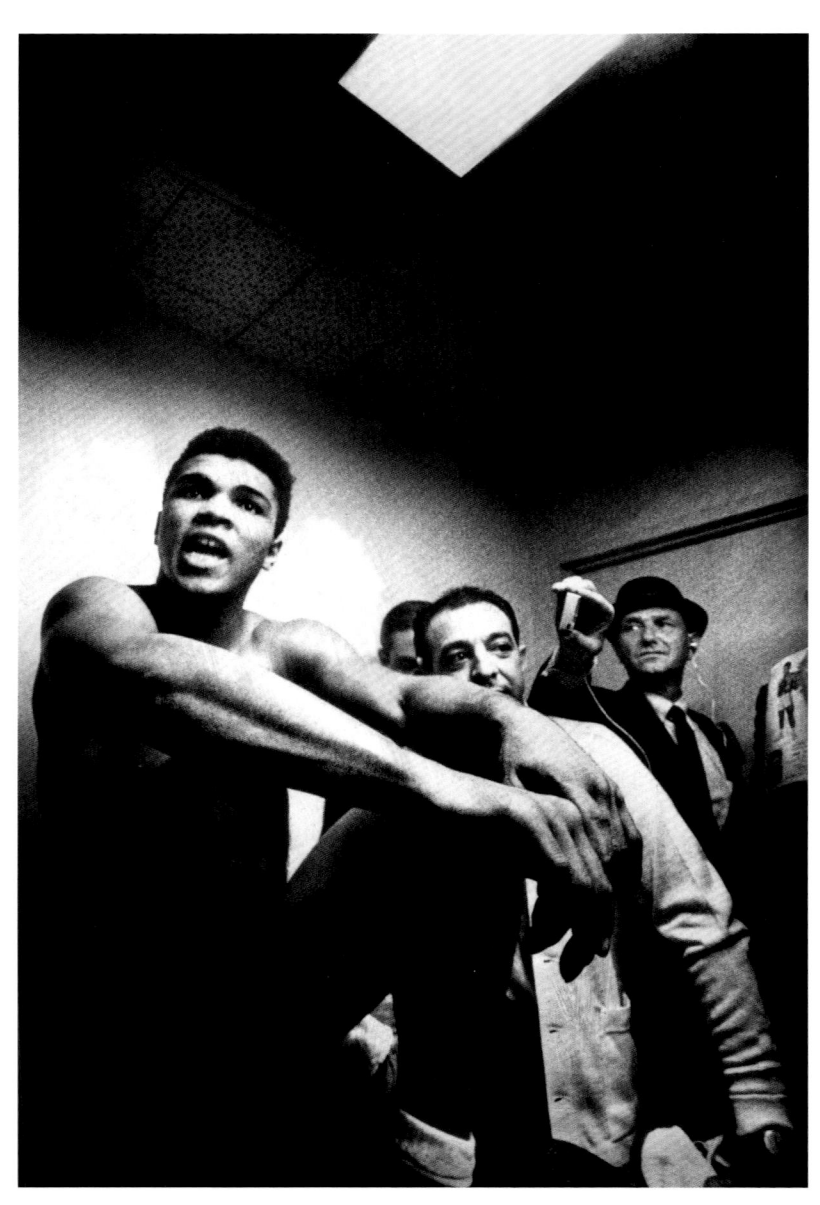

MUHAMMAD ALI

Muhammad Ali, who won this fight against former heavyweight champ Floyd Patterson in Las Vegas in 1965, was the bigger man, flashier, more confident: king of his world. The self-proclaimed "Greatest" had recently converted to Islam and changed his name from Cassius Clay. By the time of the "Thrilla in Manila" in 1975, Ali had forever changed the way everyone looked at boxing.

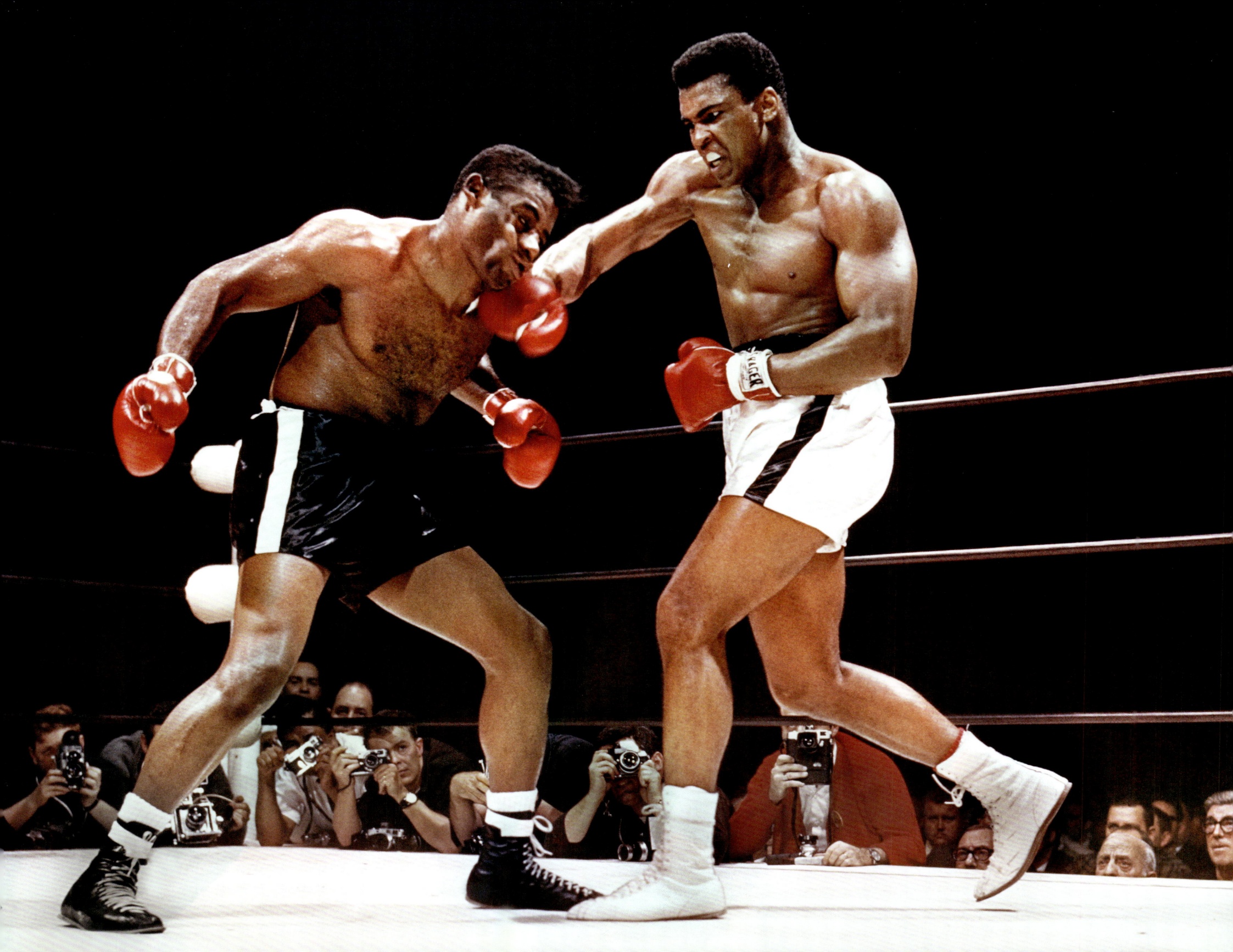

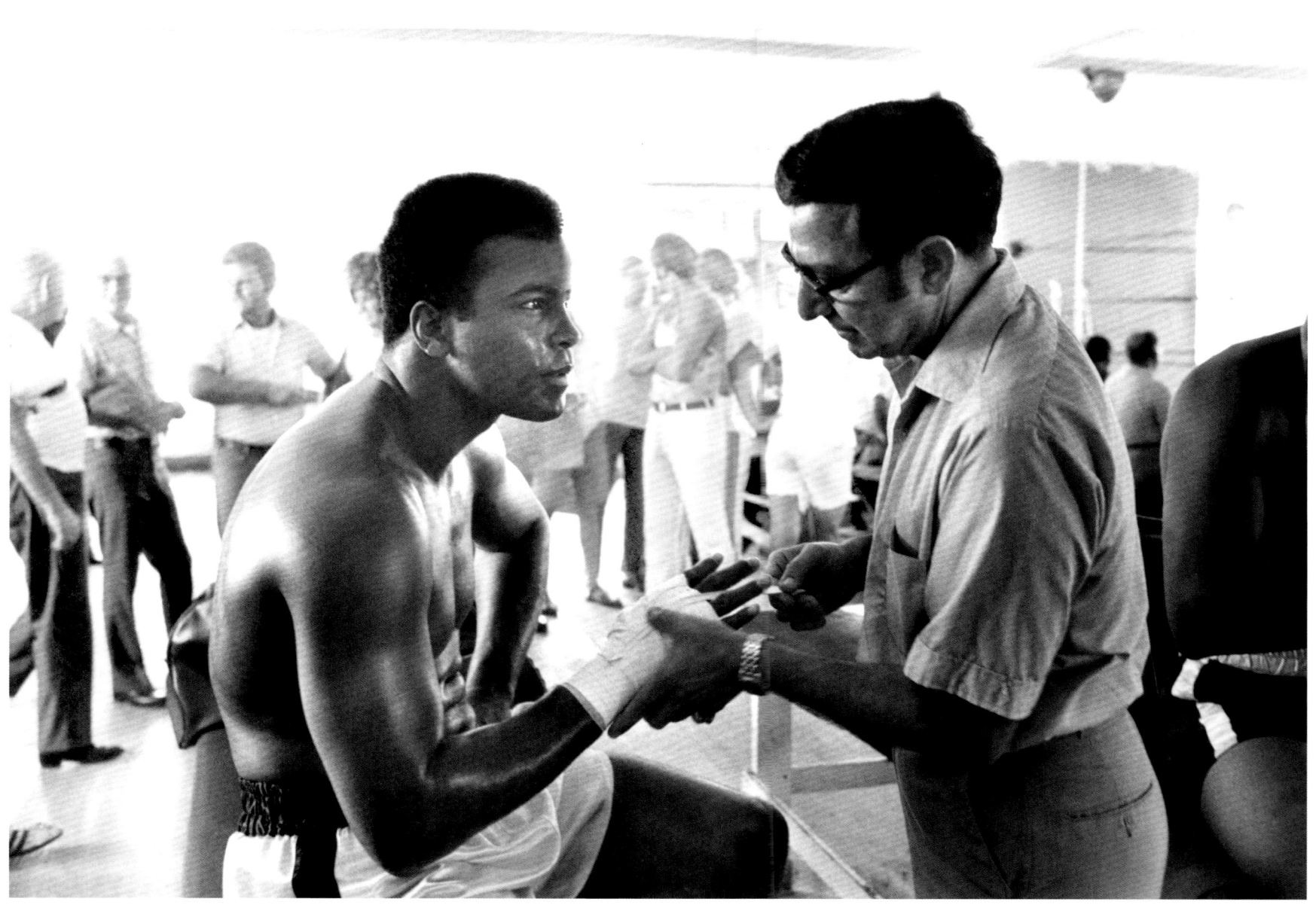

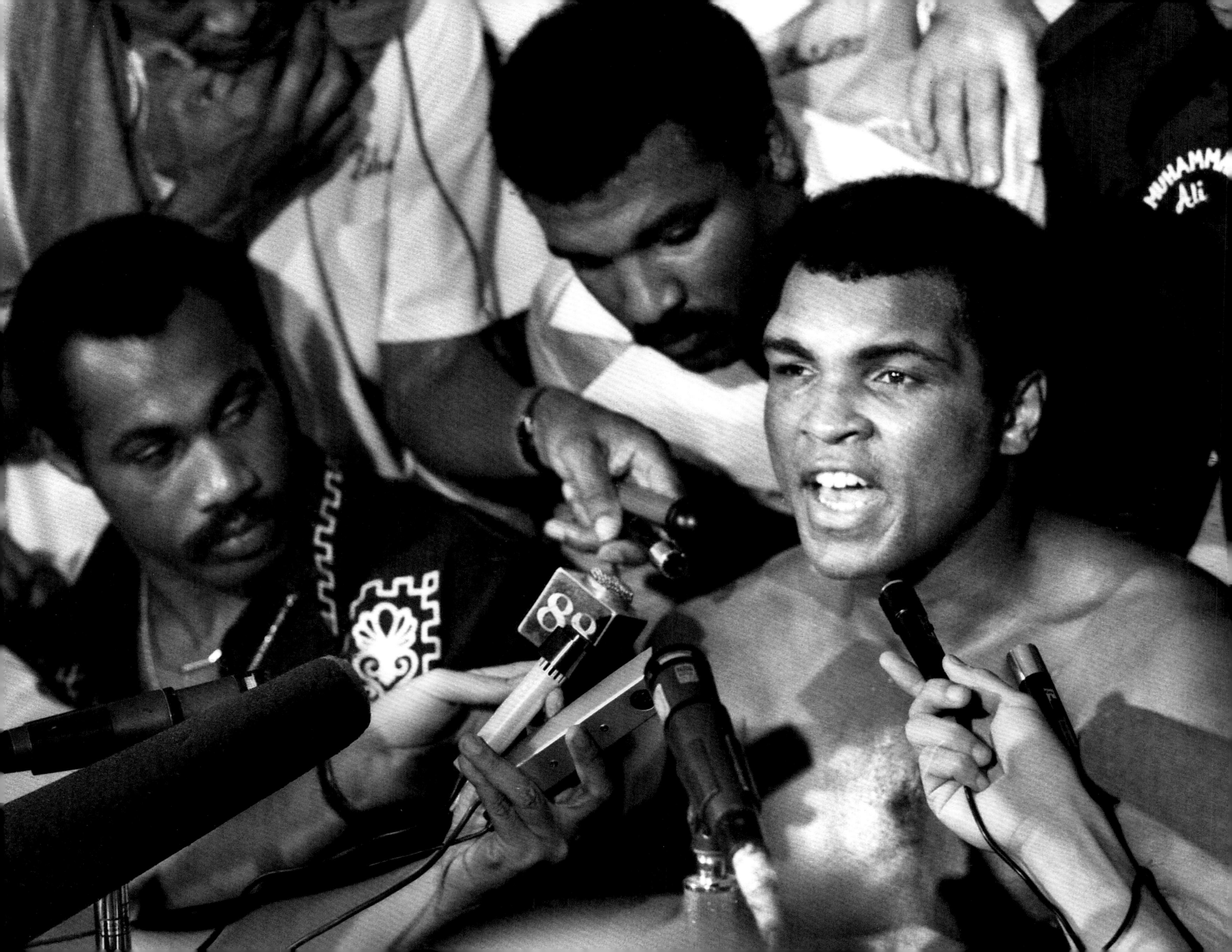

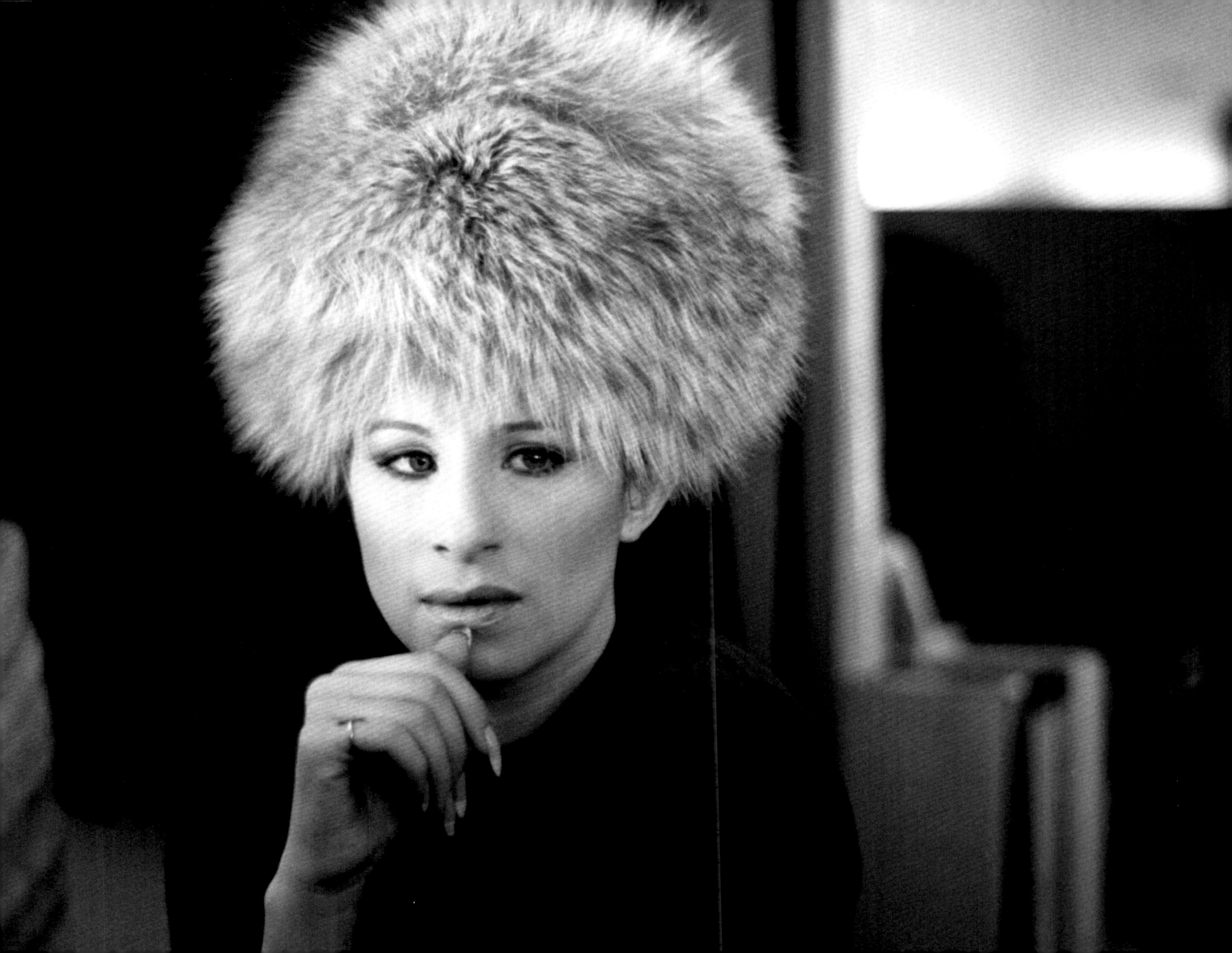

BARBRA STREISAND

Filming for *On A Clear Day You Can See Forever* began in 1968, soon after the phenomenal success of Barbra Streisand's big-screen debut in *Funny Girl*. *Life* magazine had guaranteed her a cover with her costar, Yves Montand, but she never showed up for the shoot. "Don't you understand," Barbra later explained, "a picture of me with Montand becomes old when this film is over, but a picture of me alone can always be used."

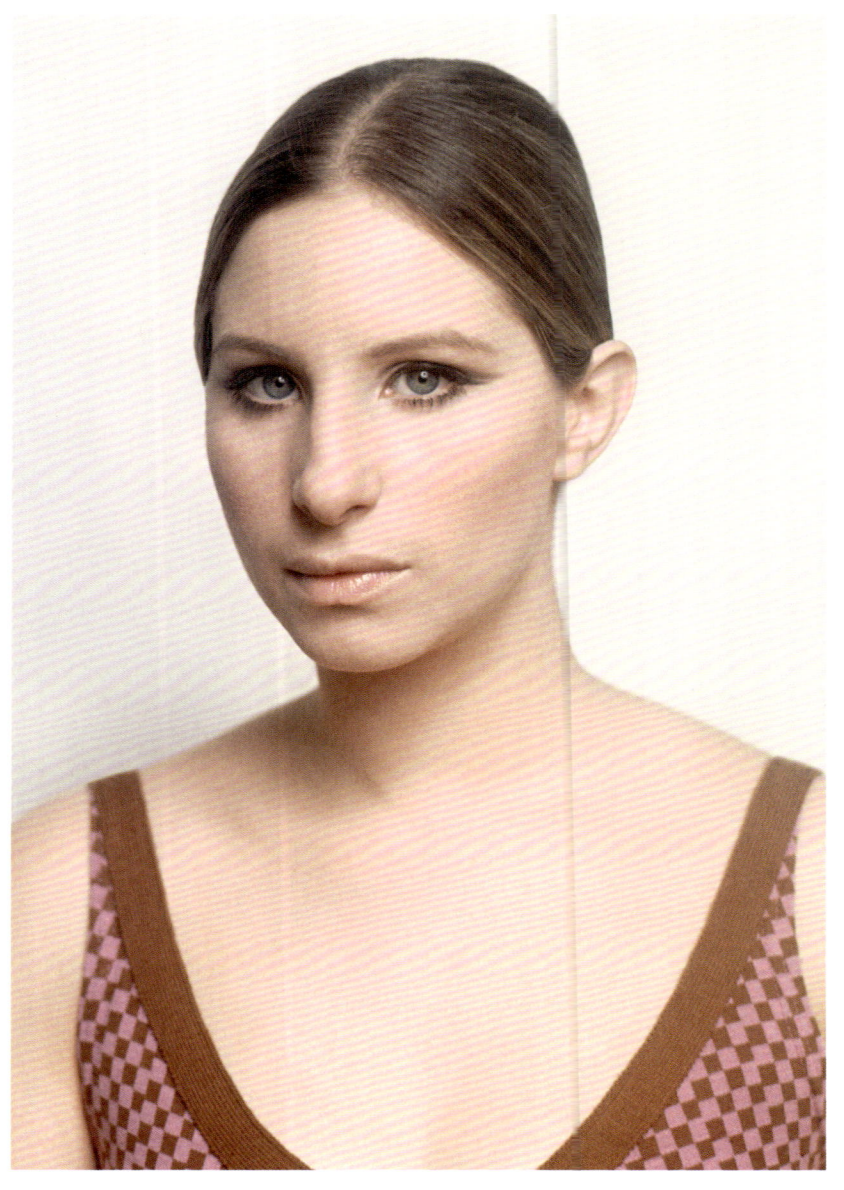

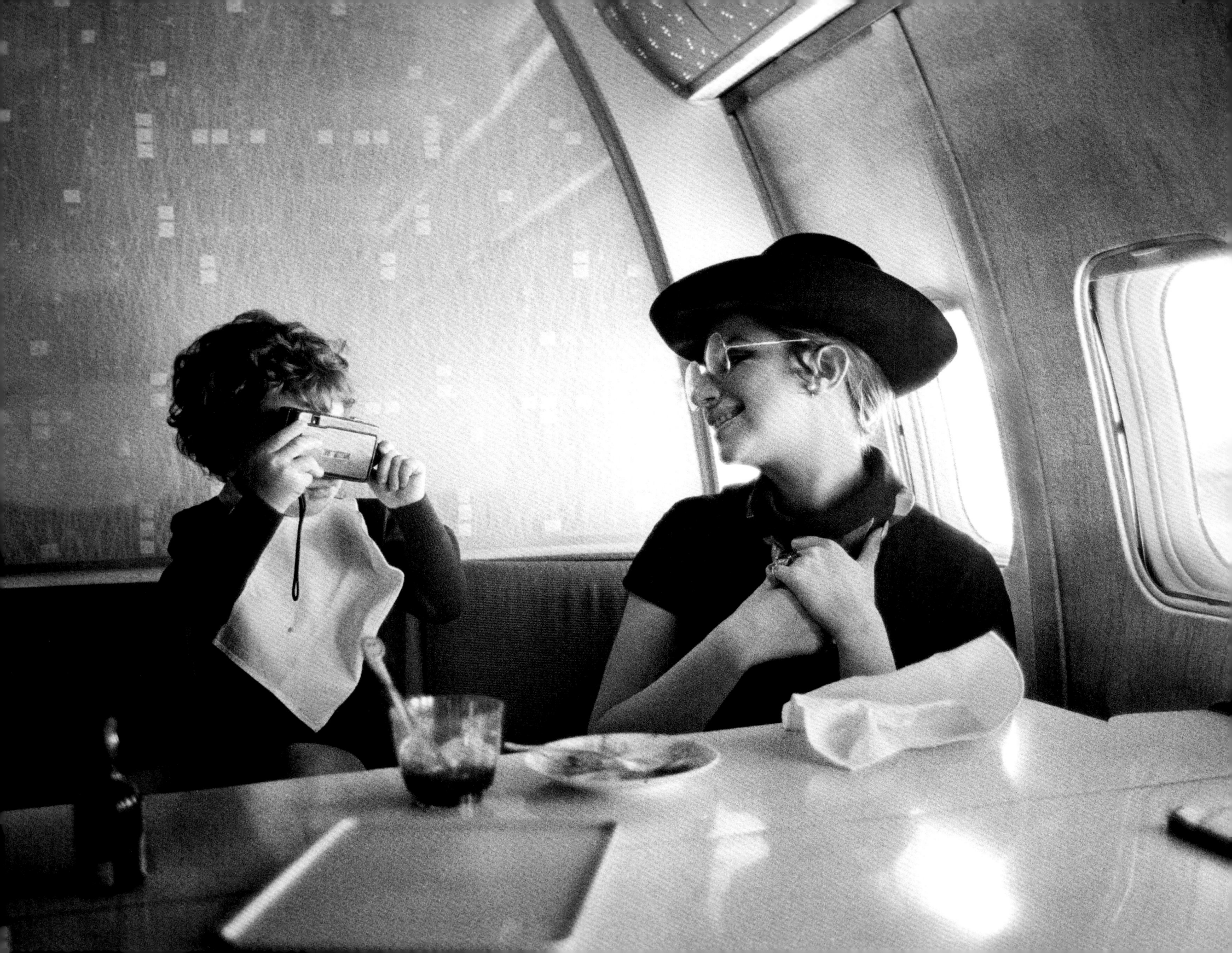

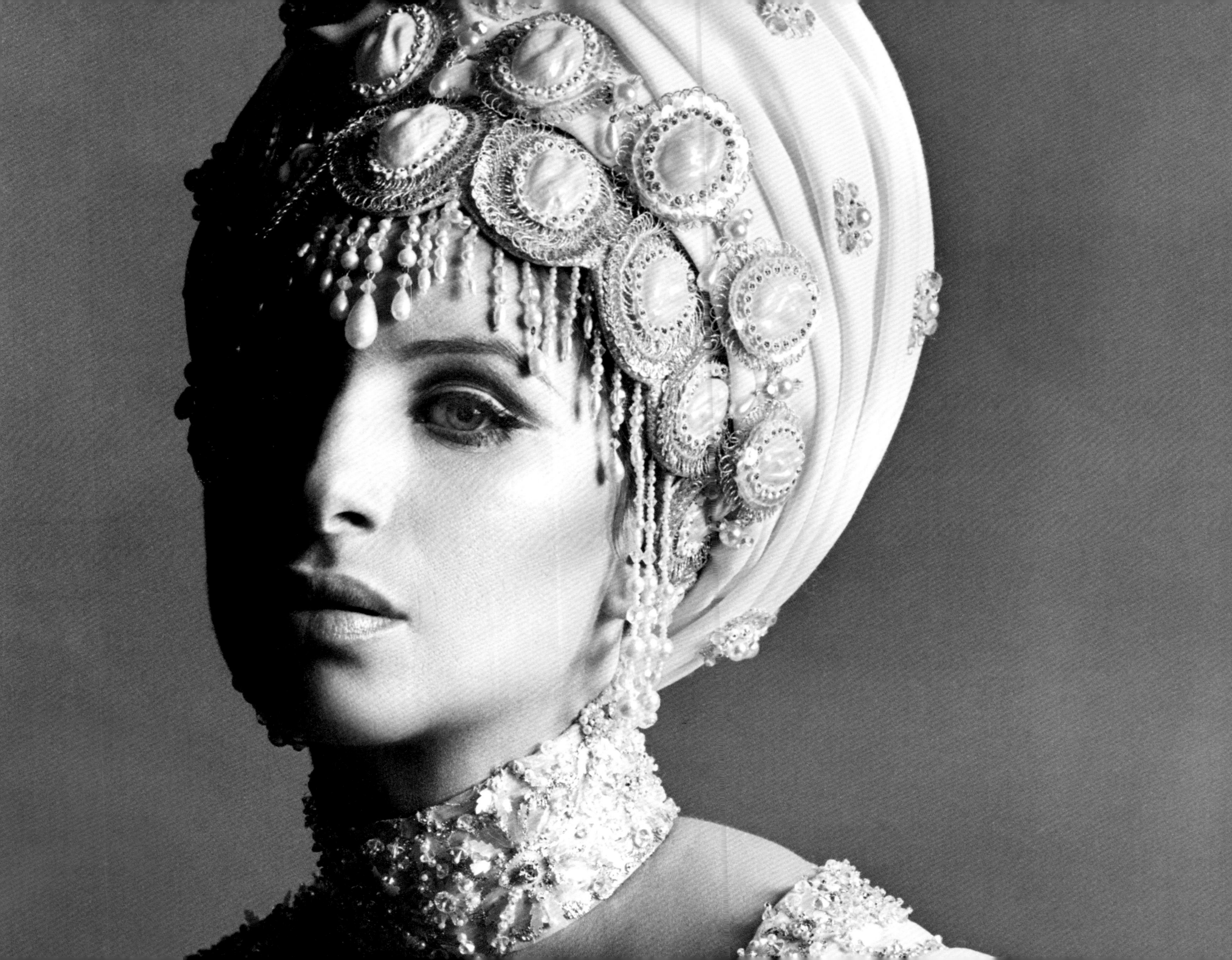

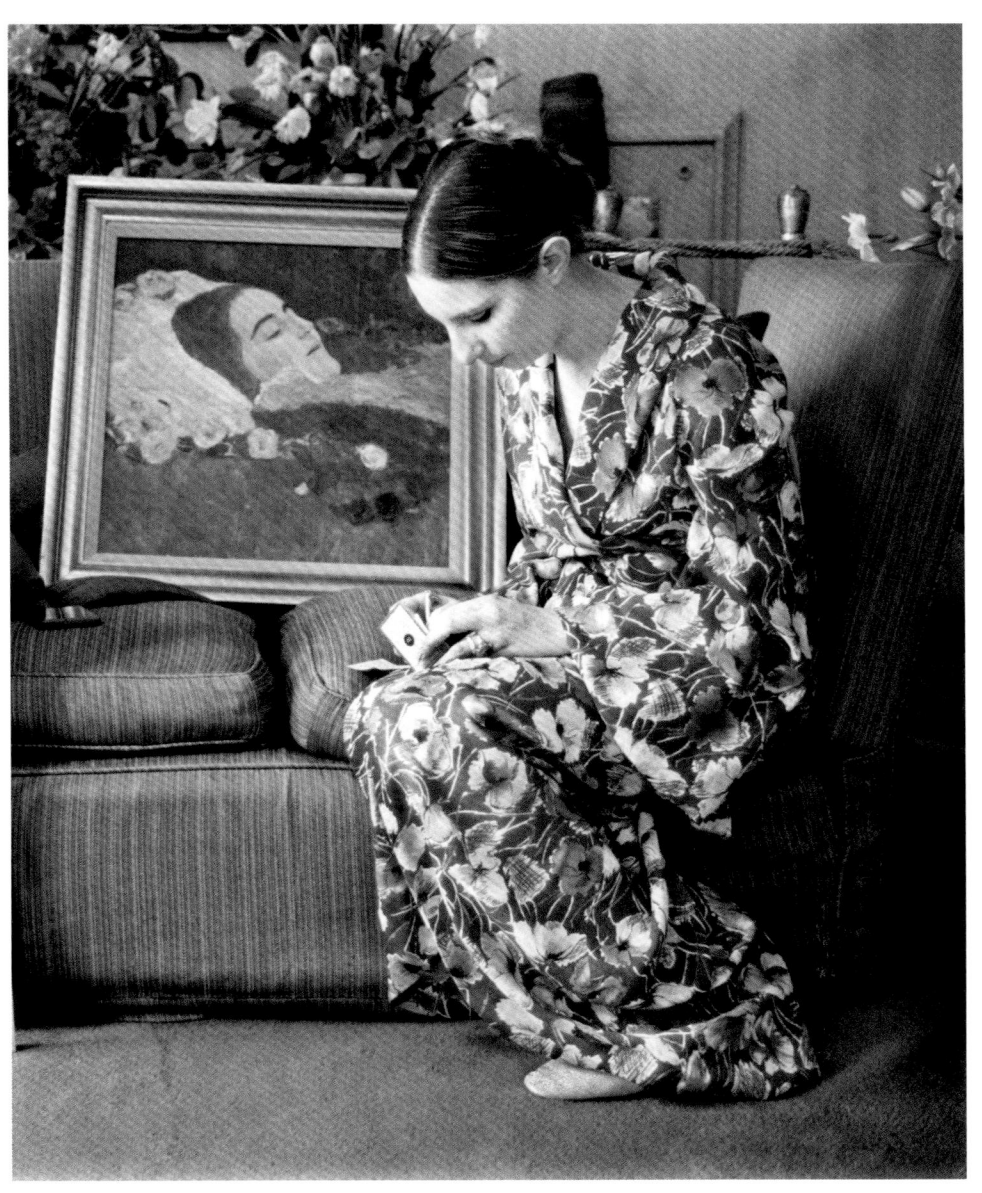

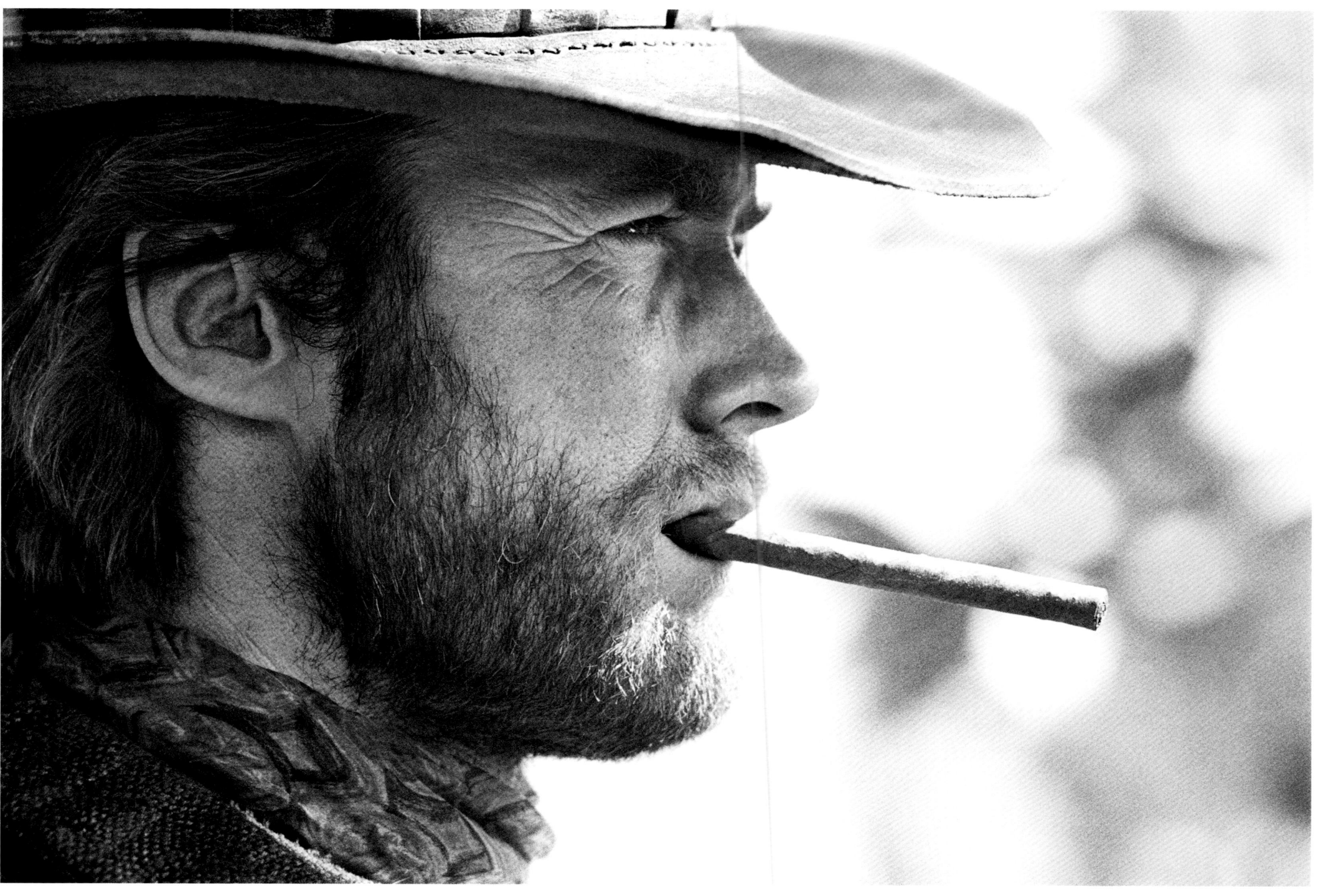

LEGENDS

I loved parachuting into someone's life and being able to tell a story with a few images. Since I was based in Los Angeles throughout the Sixties, many of my assignments were to cover Hollywood. Clint Eastwood, James Earl Jones, Alfred Hitchcock, and Sophia Loren were legends in their own right, but Buster Keaton, then at the nadir in the arc of his career, was my most fascinating and complex subject.

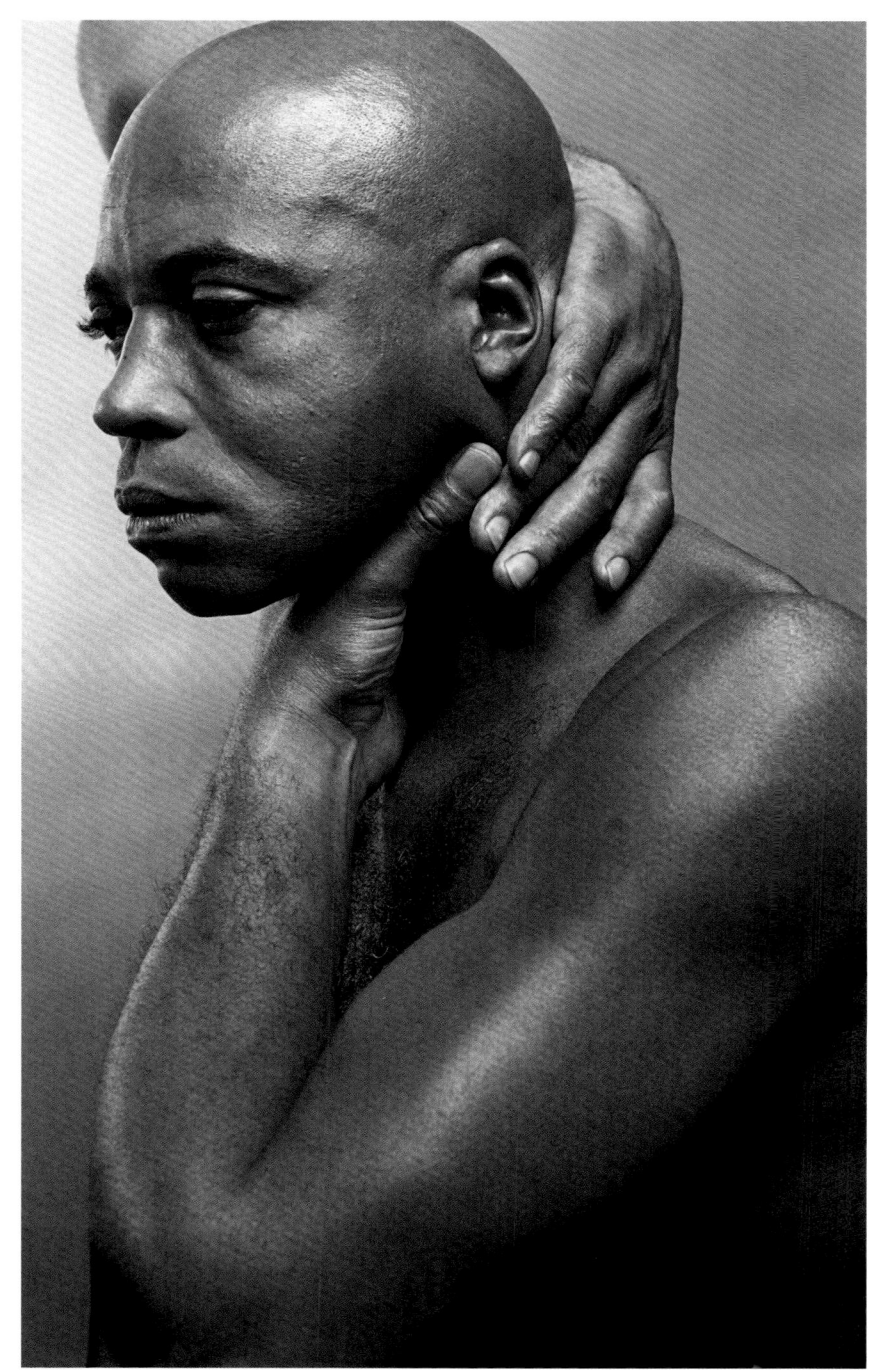

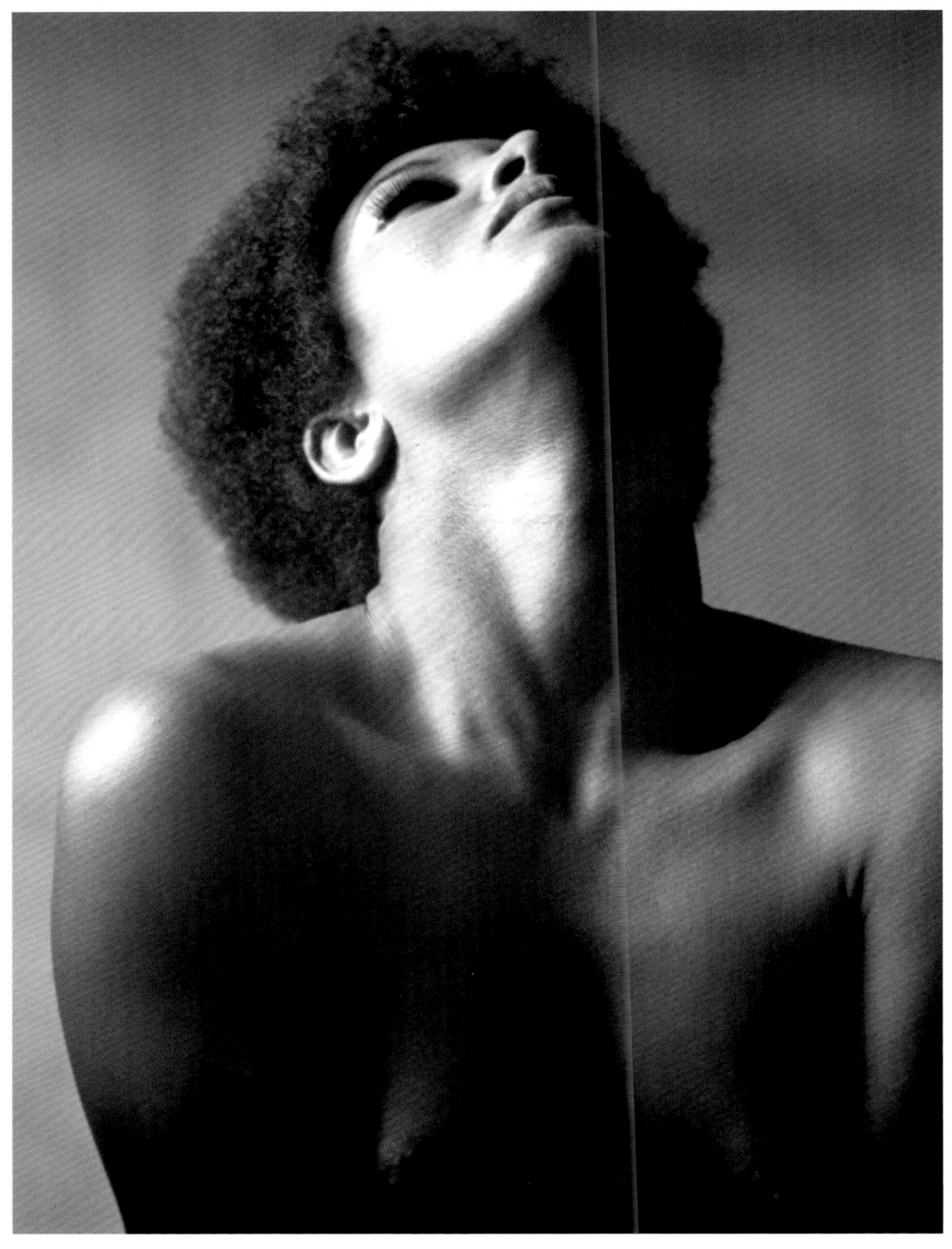

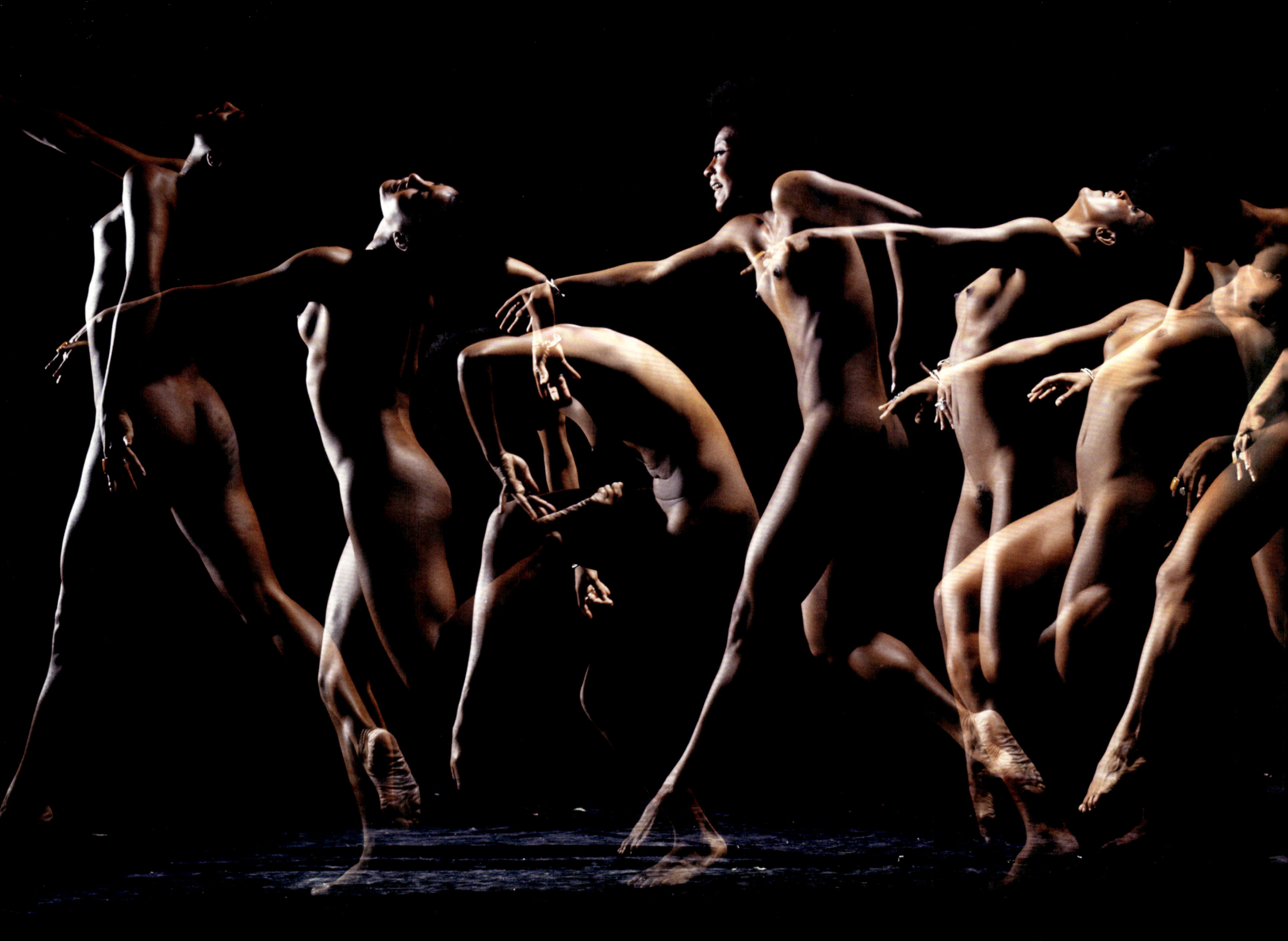

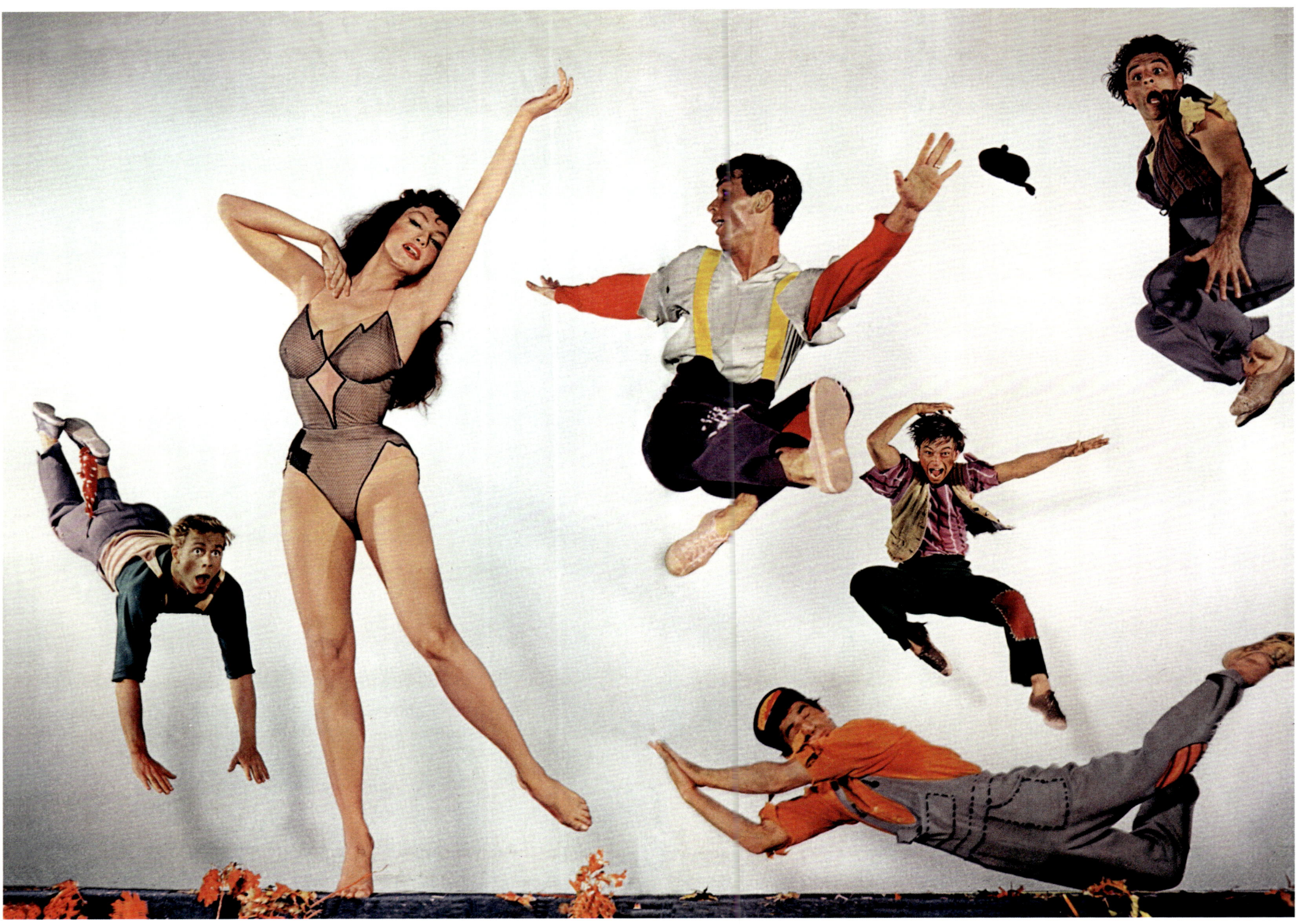

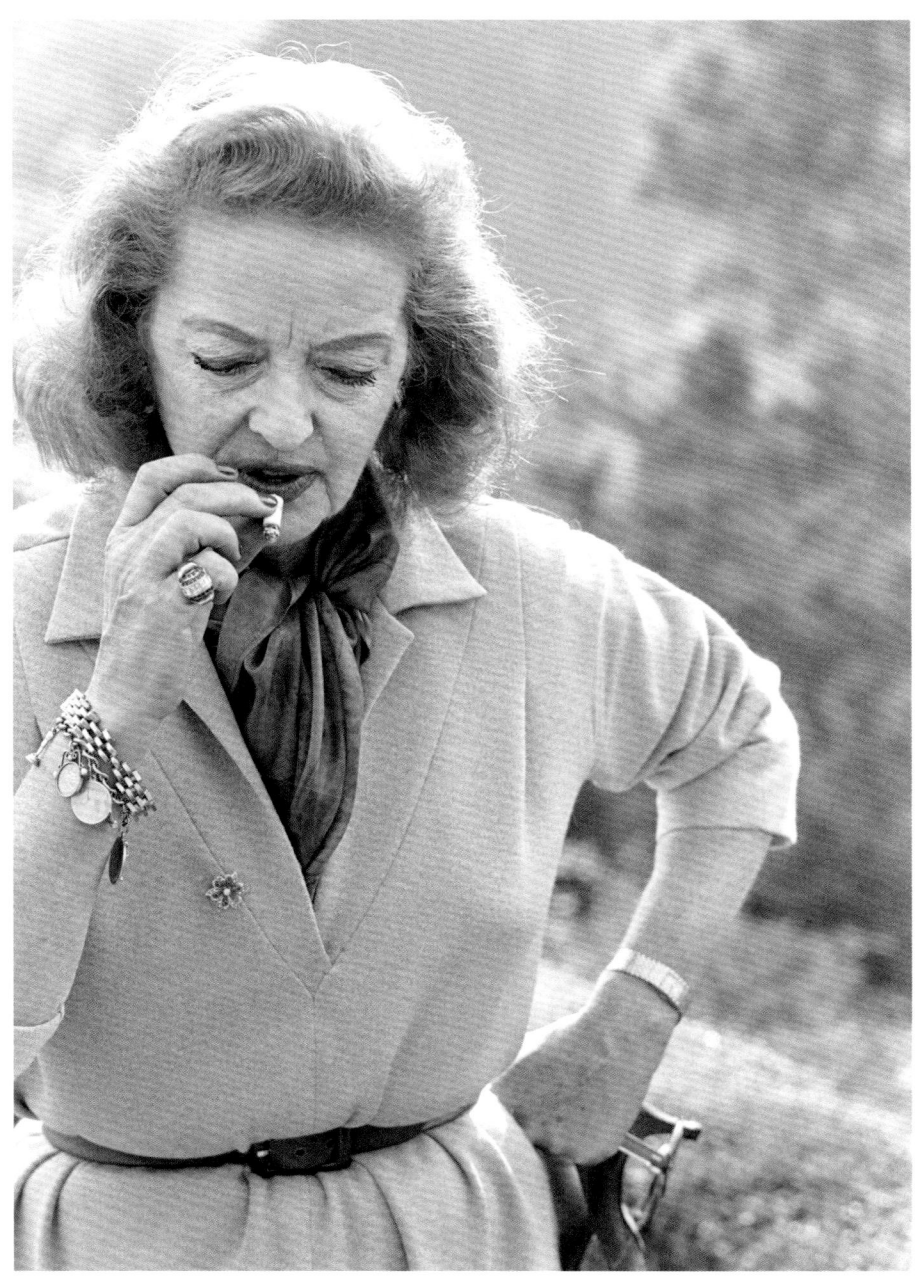

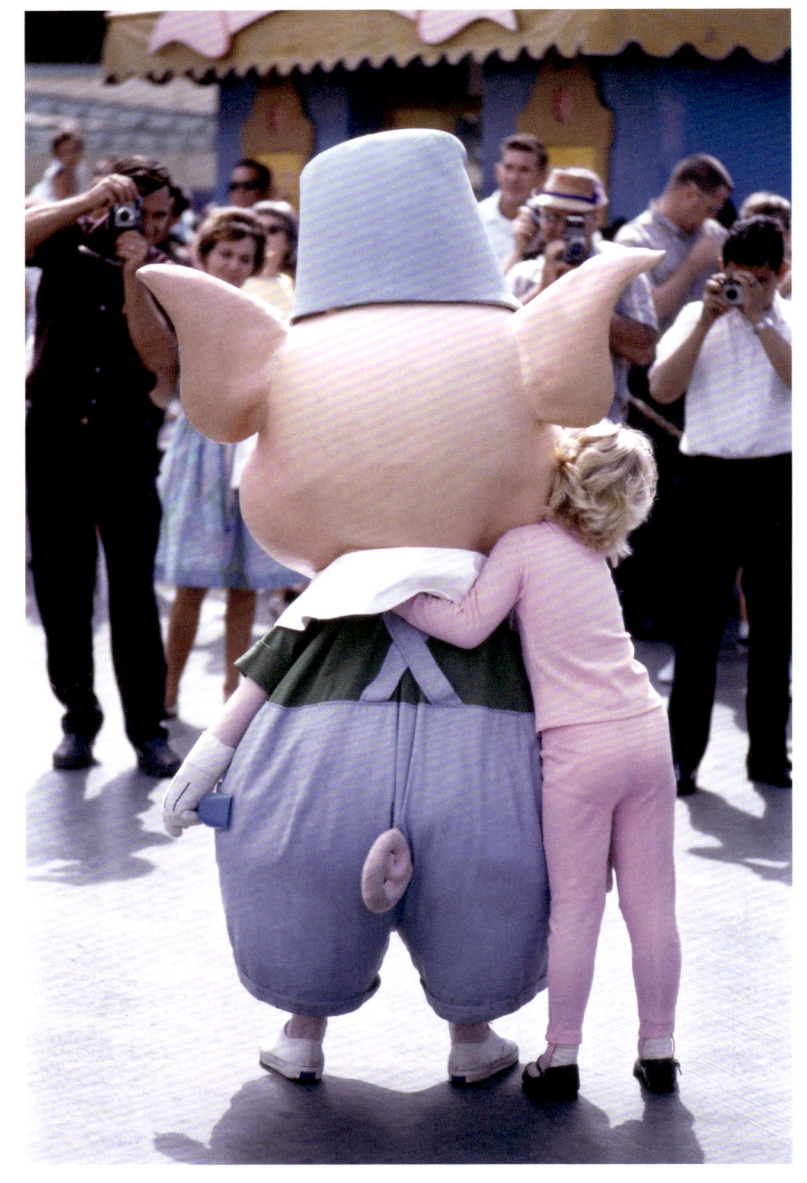

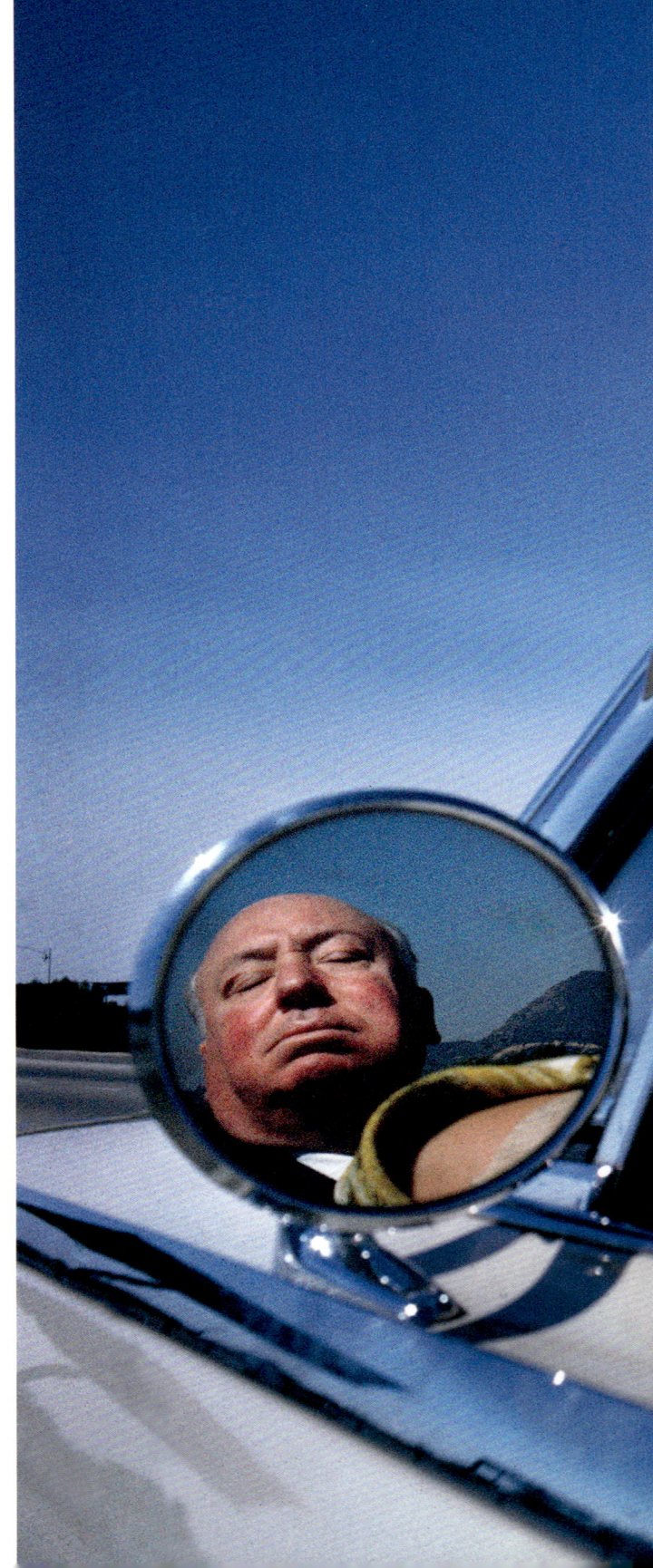

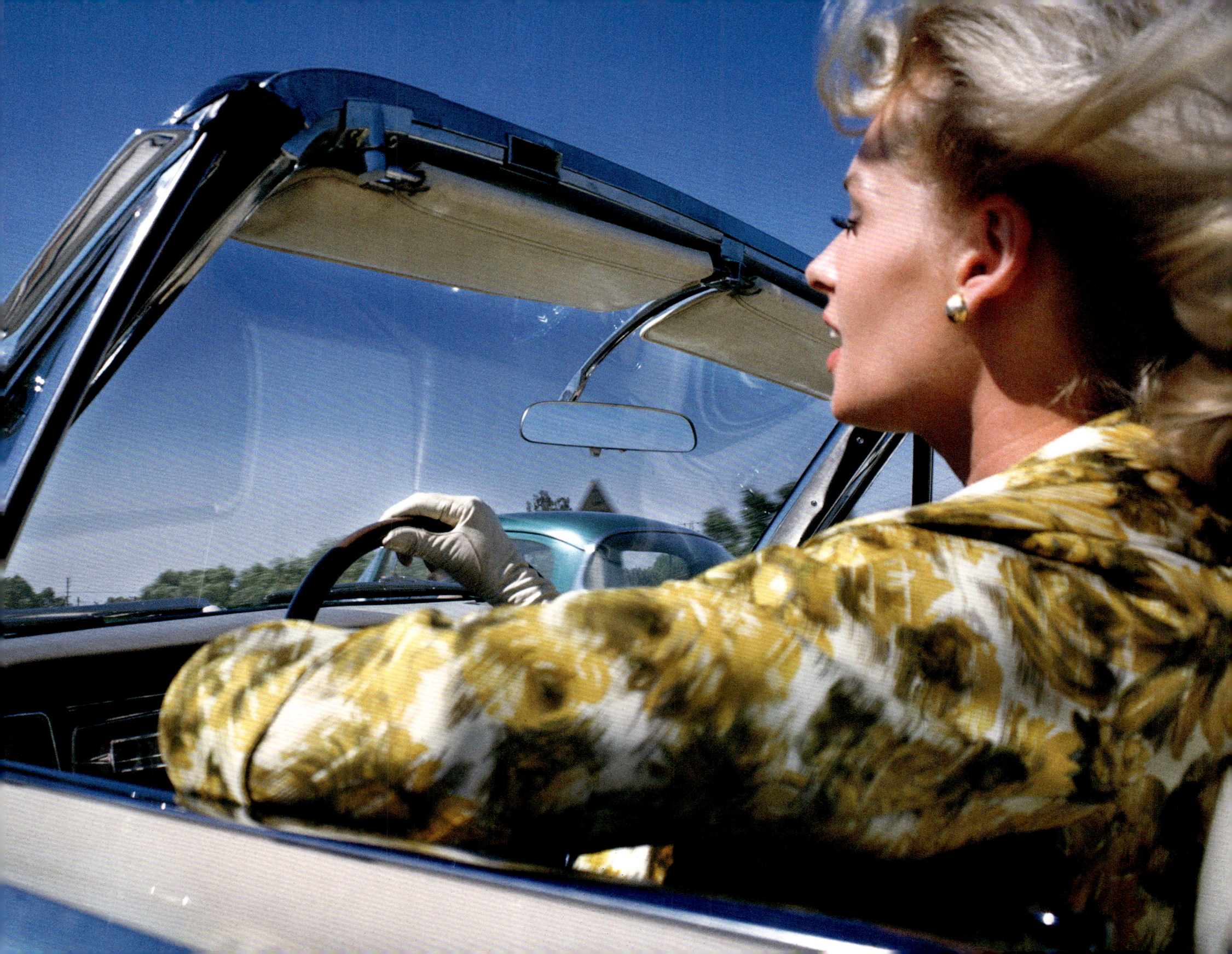

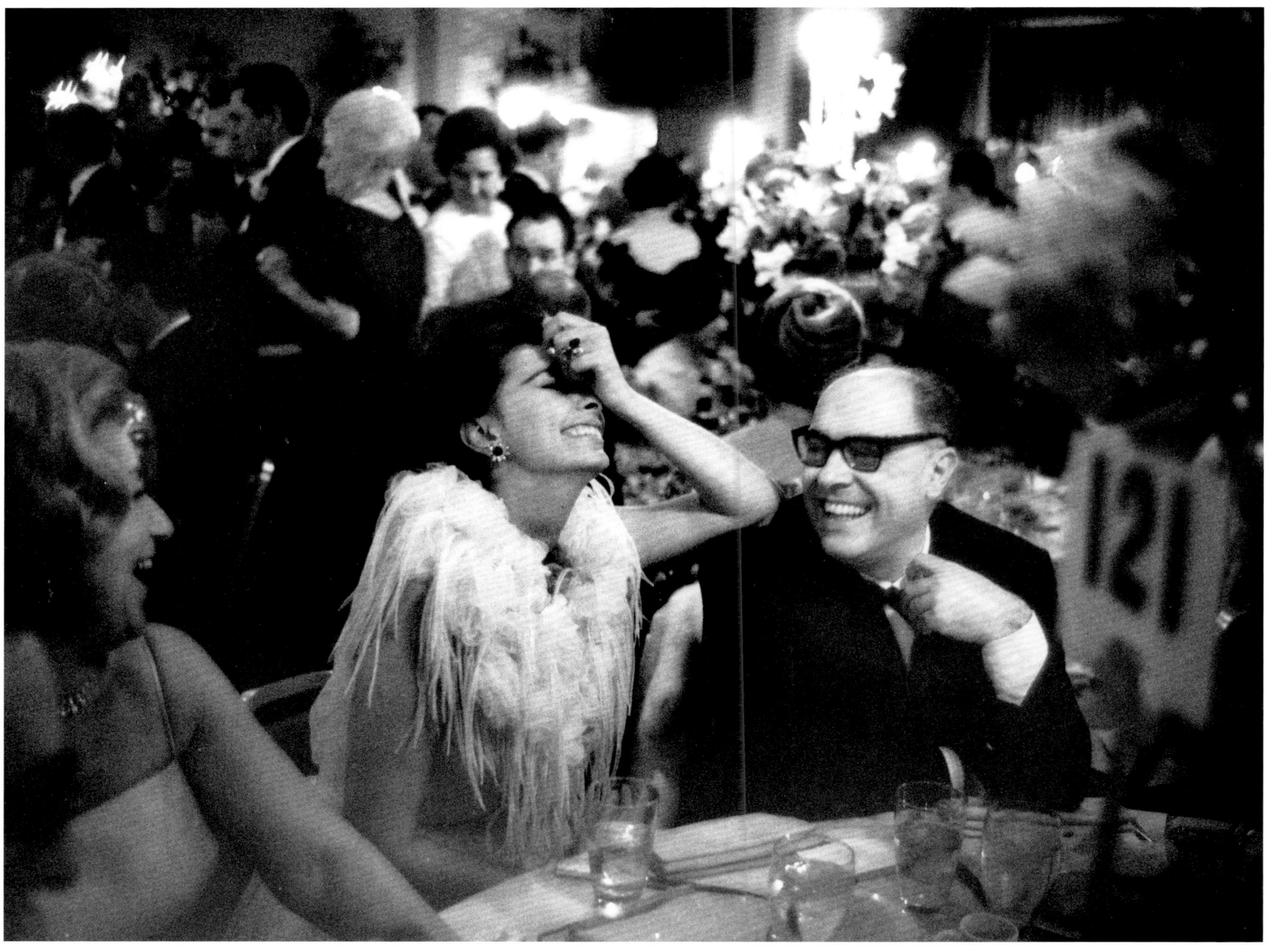

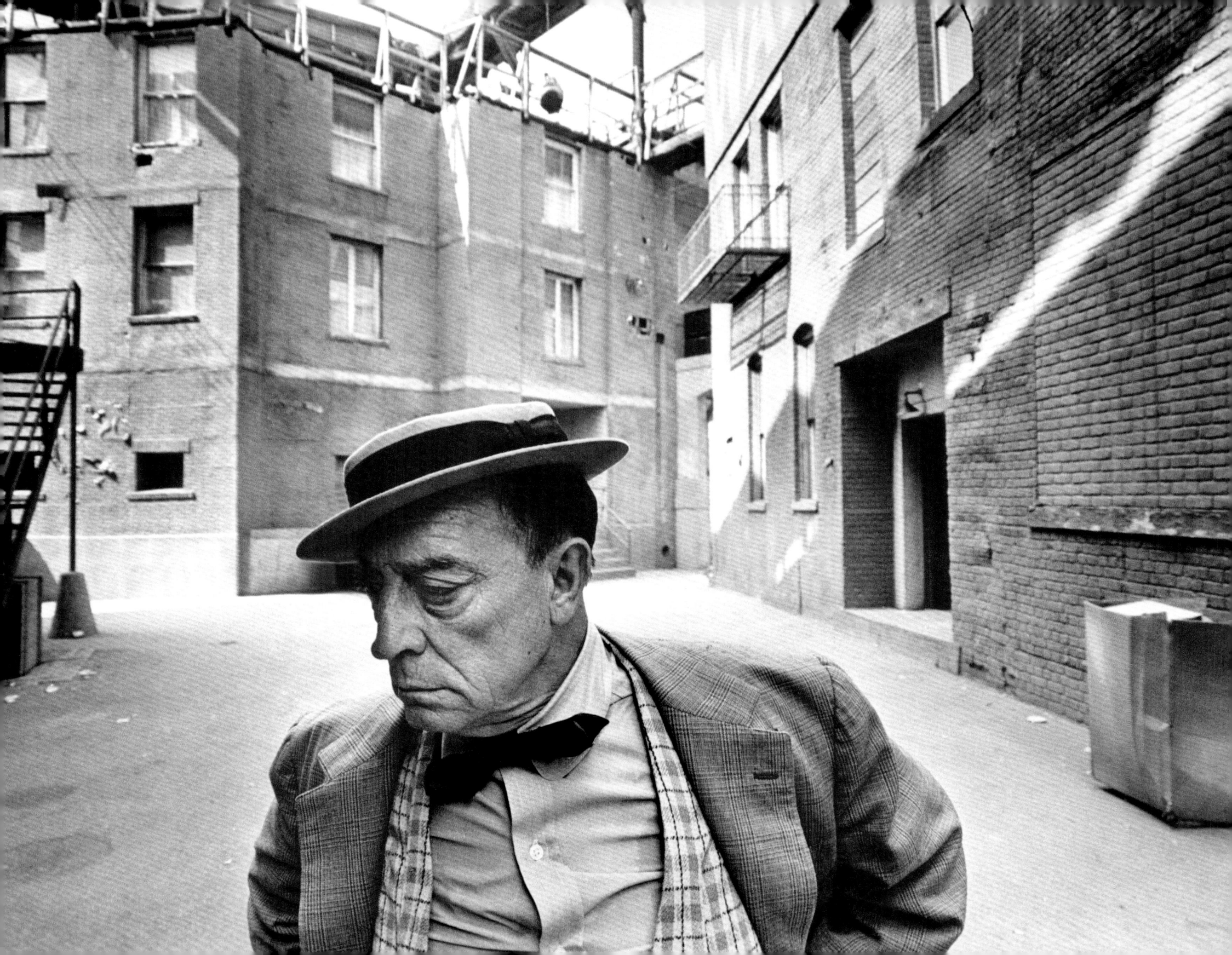

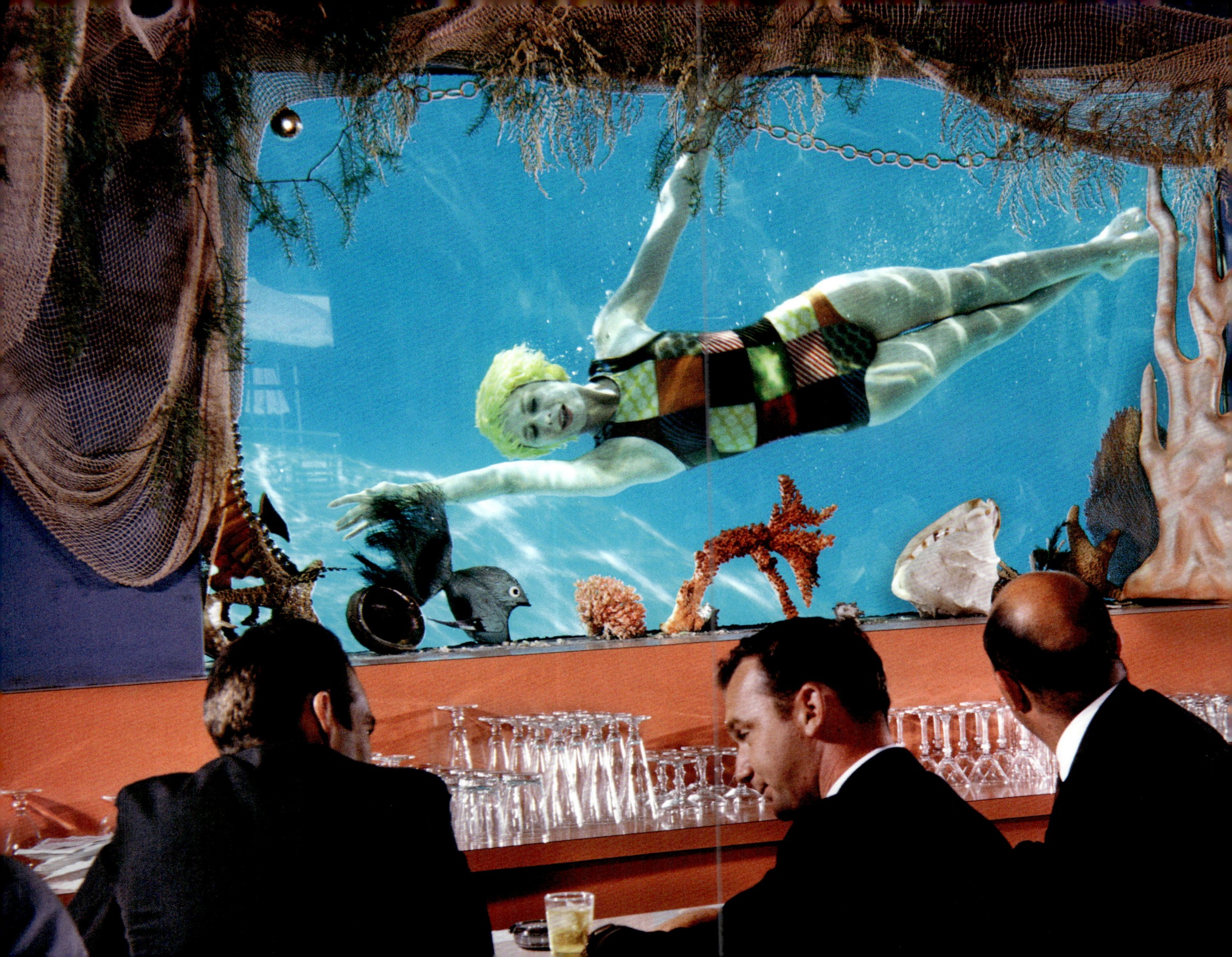

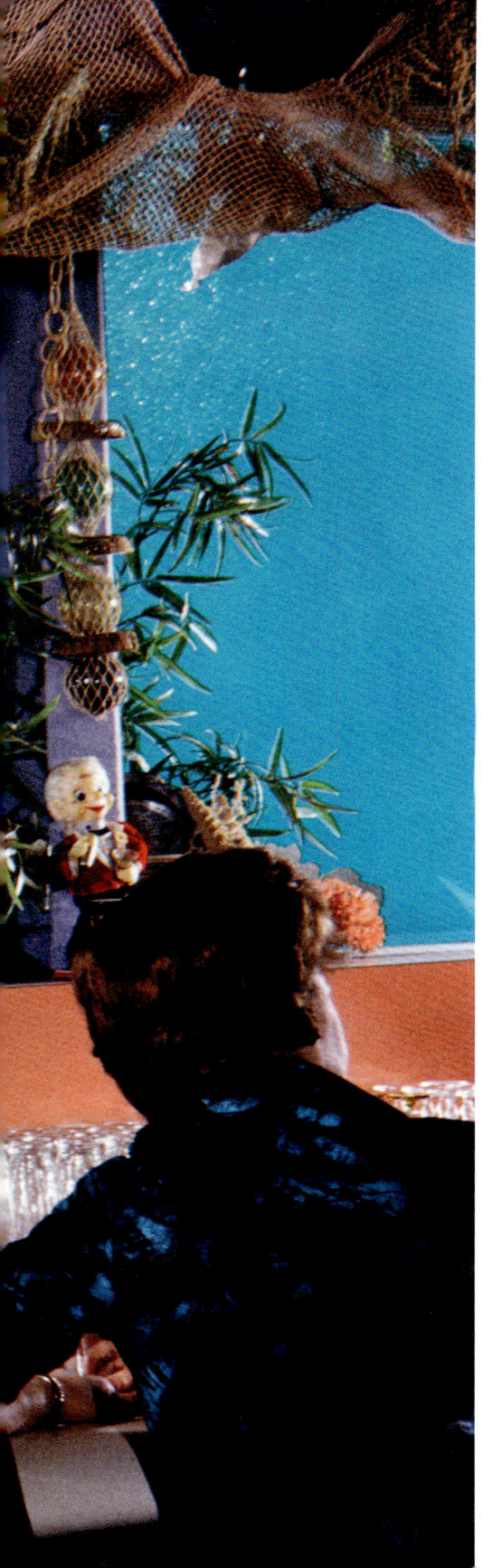

CALIFORNIA

In Southern California where I lived, beaches and pools were a go-to location for photoshoots with celebrities and models. So, when Berry Gordy, the president of Motown, asked me to take some pictures of a new band from Gary, Indiana, on their first visit to California, to the beach it was. Little did I know that the Jackson 5 weren't just dancing to their music but with joy at seeing the ocean for the first time.

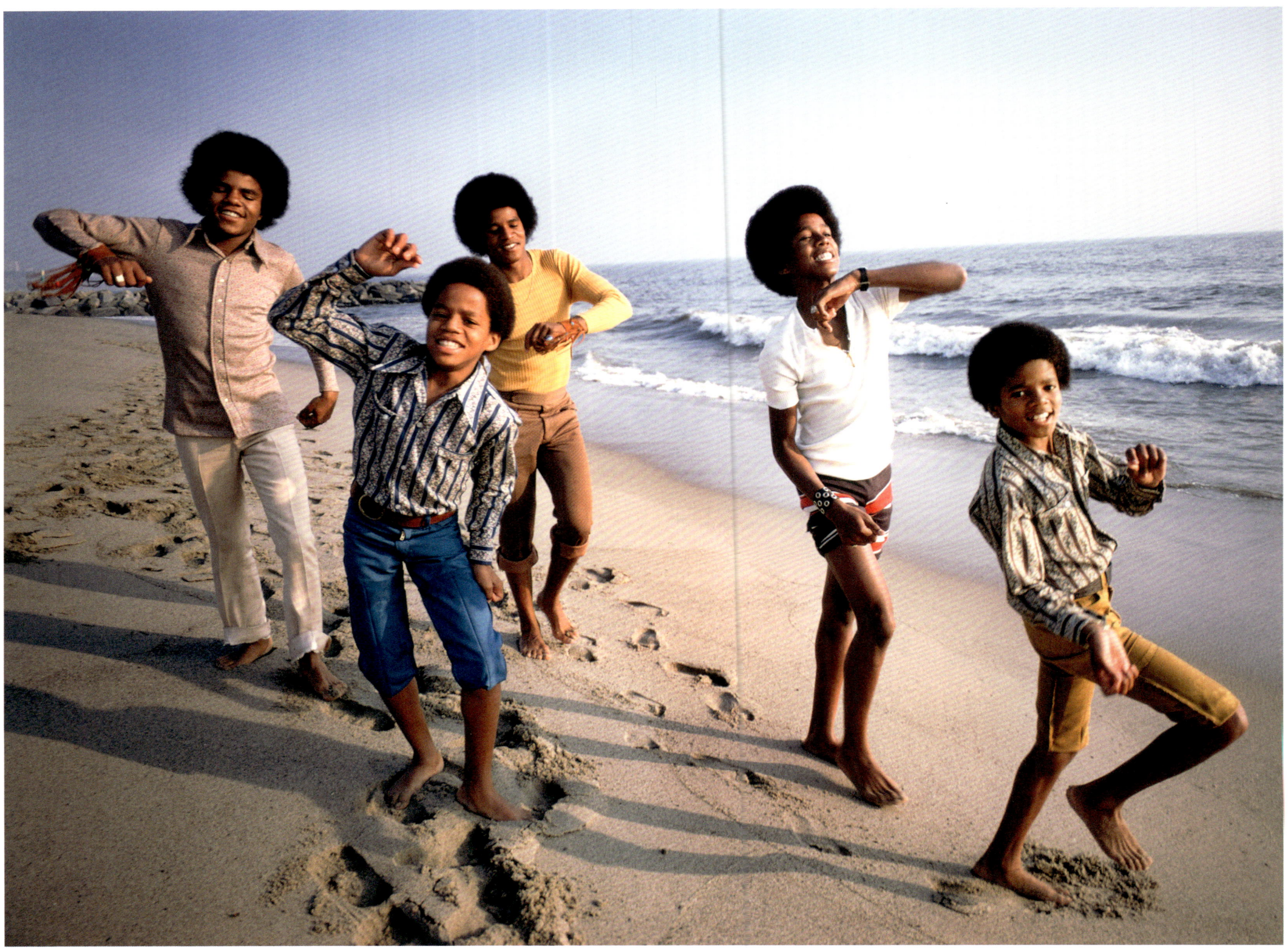

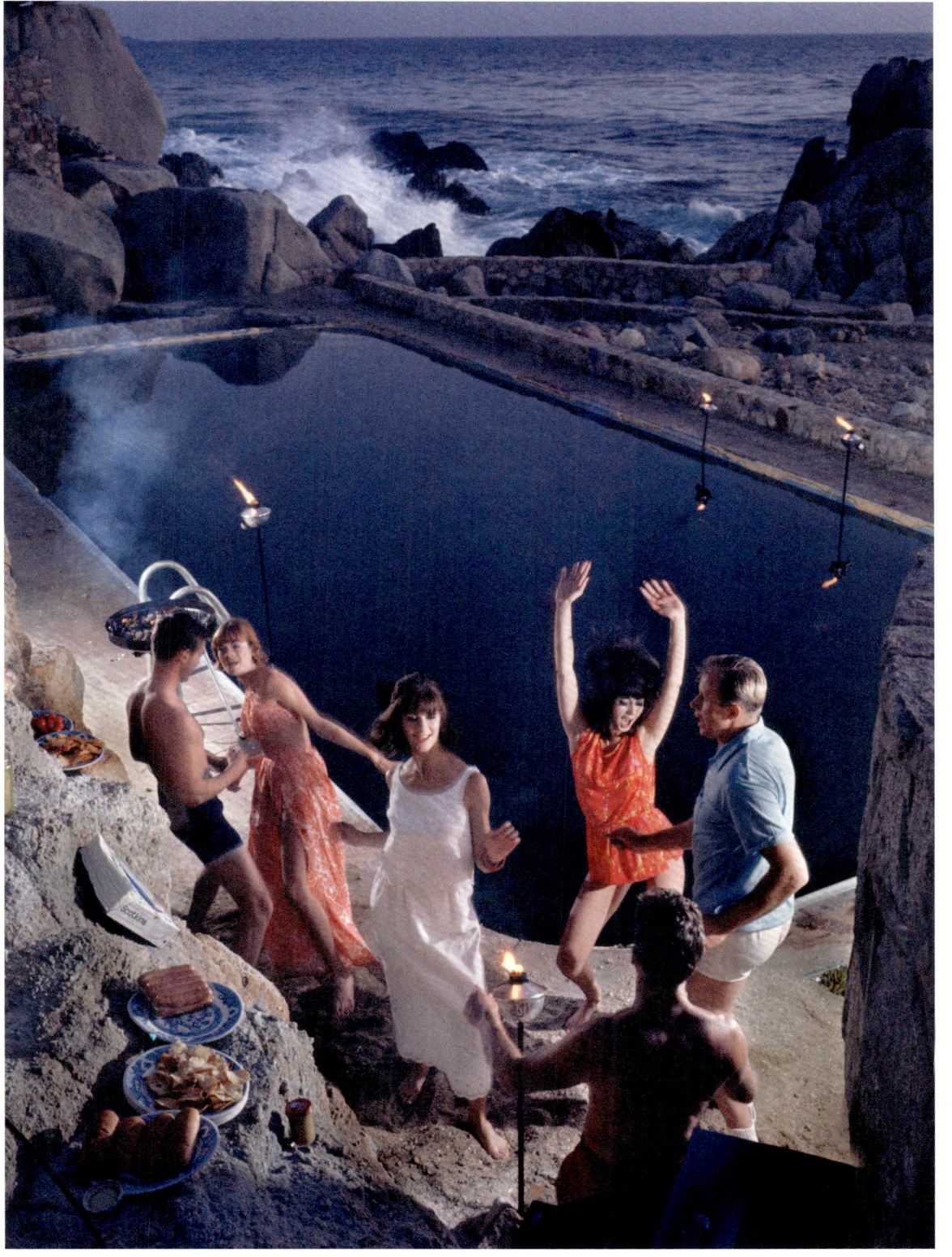

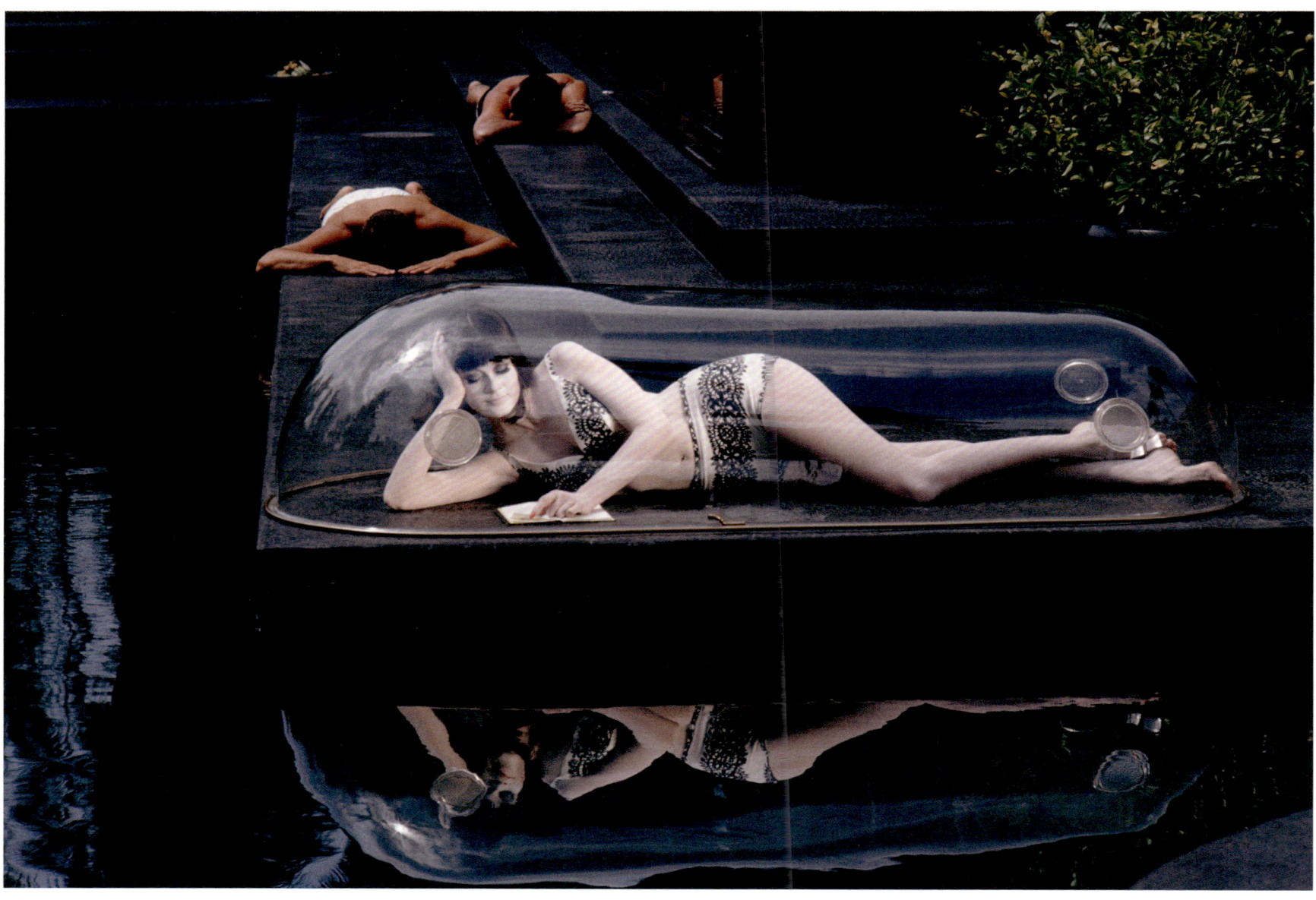

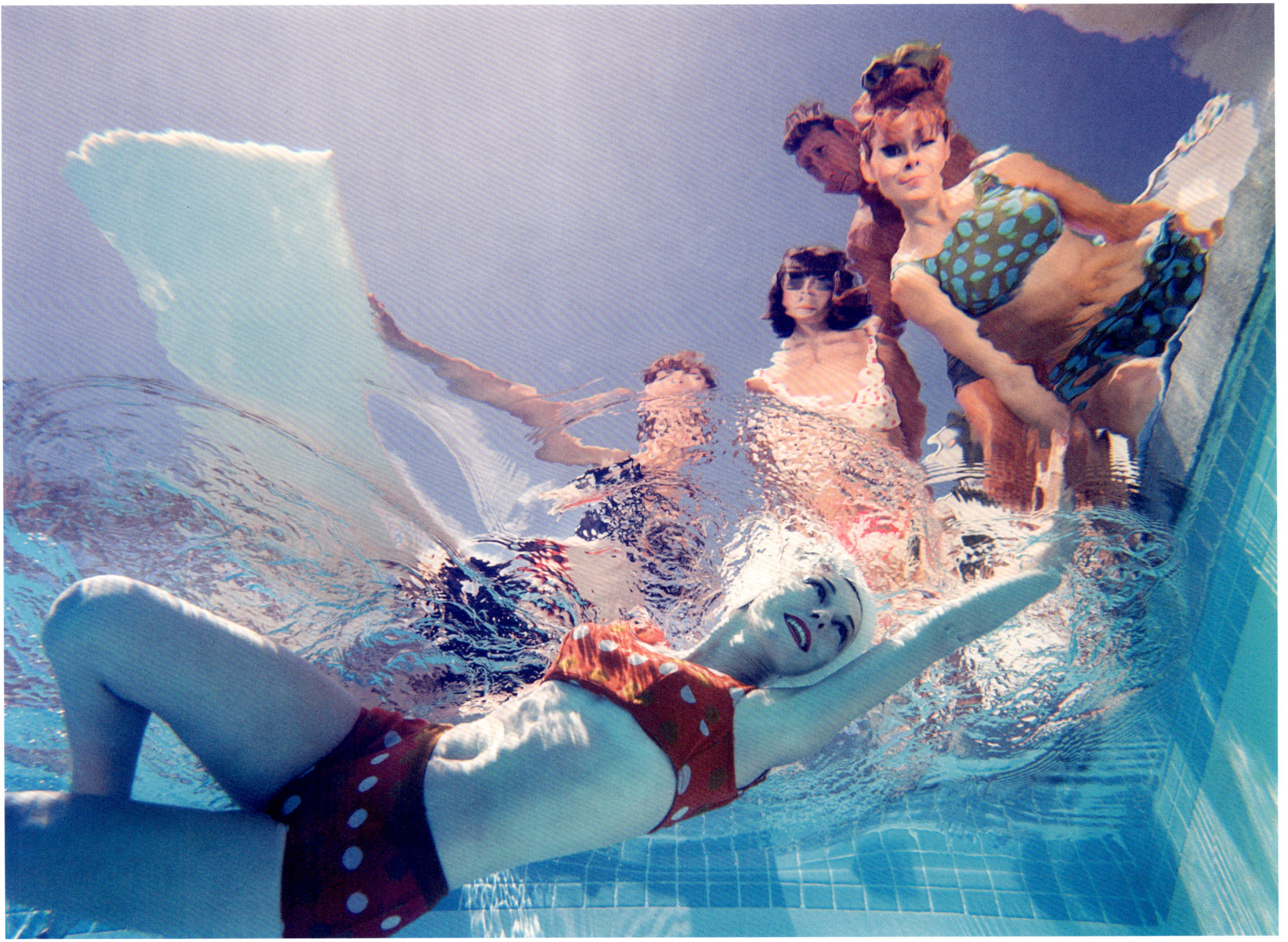

RECORD BREAKERS

My challenge in photographing sports was to illustrate what was happening from a perspective the audience could not experience. In the early Sixties, there were no windows in Olympic swimming pools, so I just put some scuba gear on, put my camera in a waterproof housing, and dove in. For other shoots, I buried my Nikons in the sand, mounted them on planes and race cars, and sat back with a remote control while my subjects broke records.

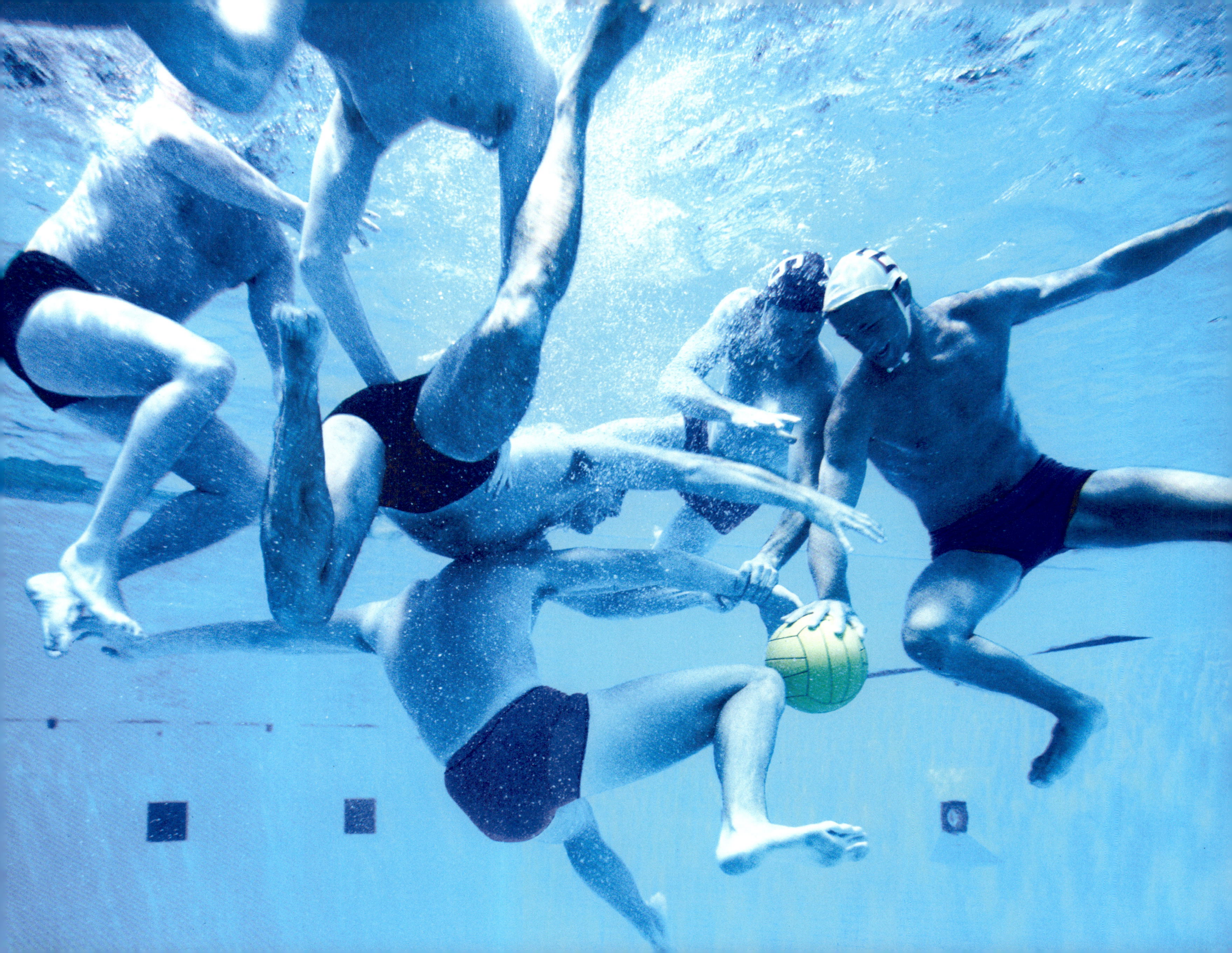

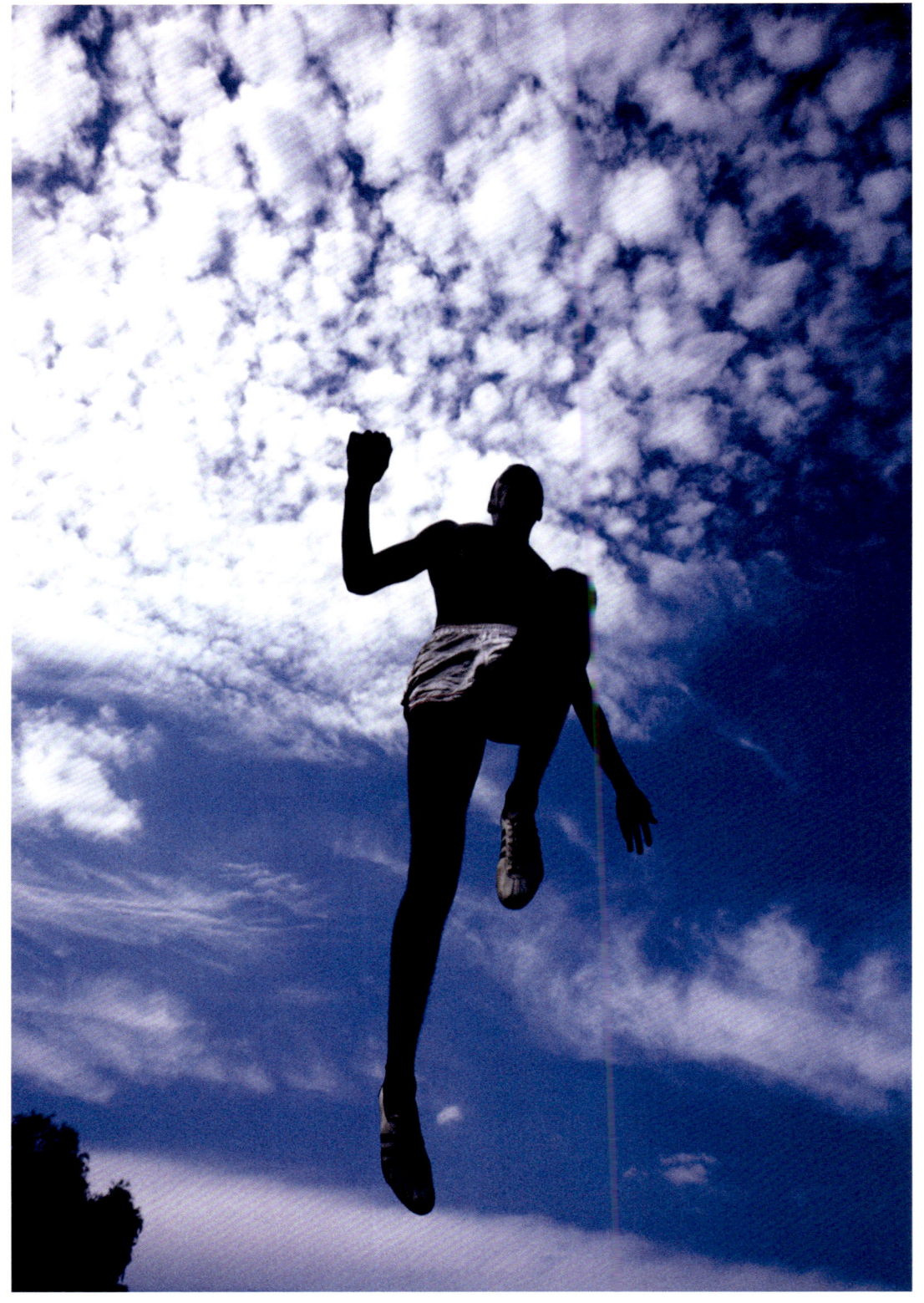

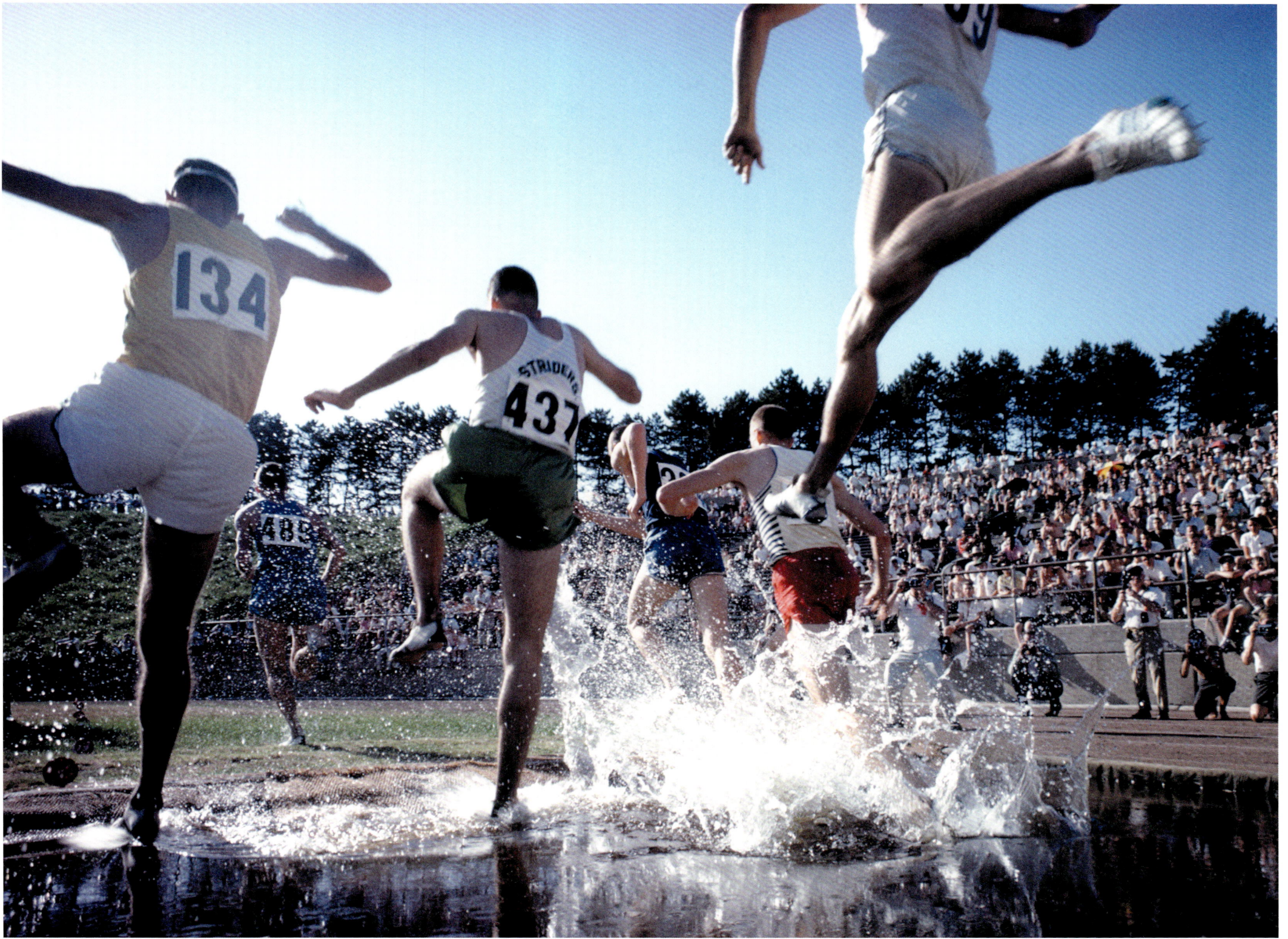

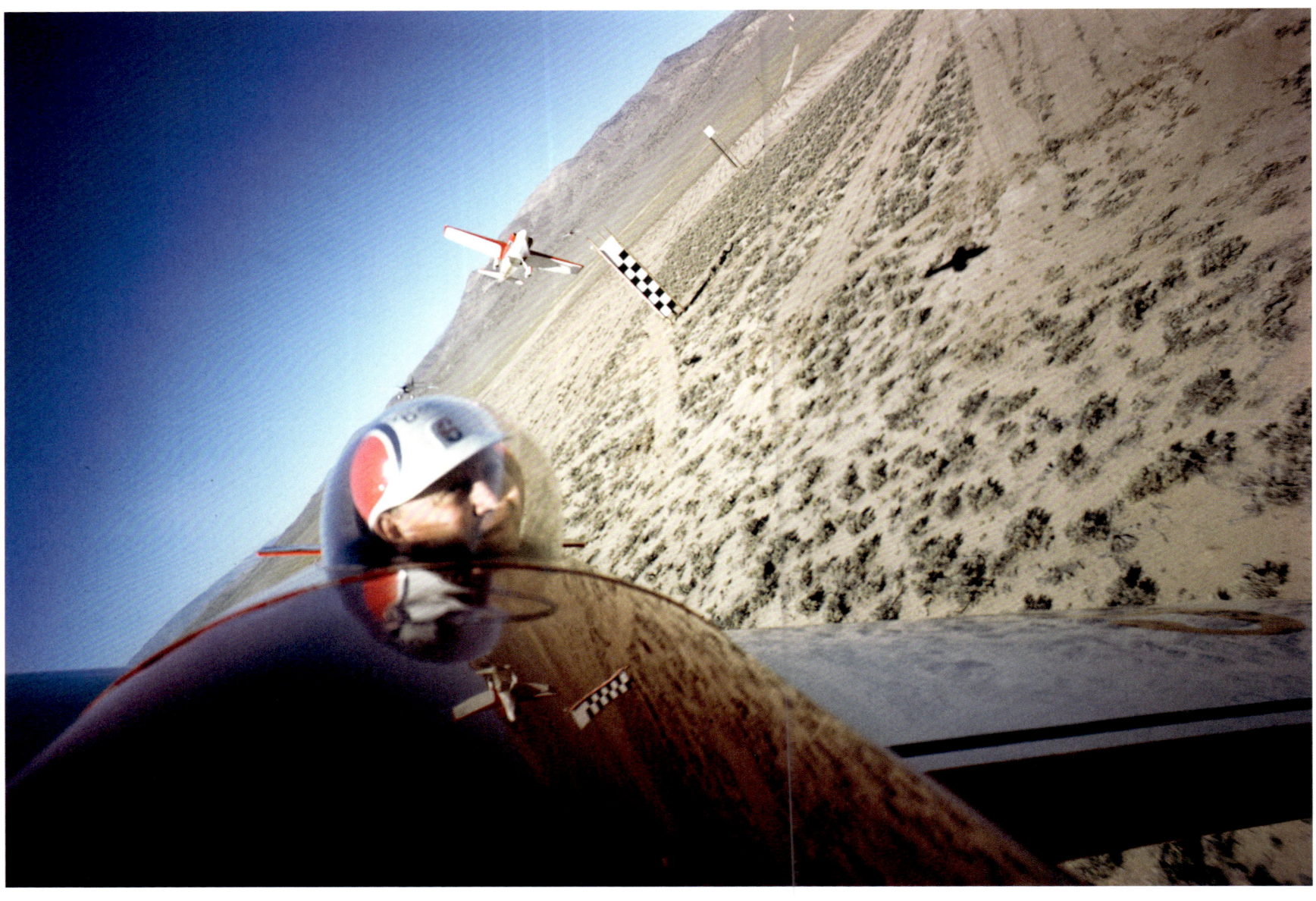

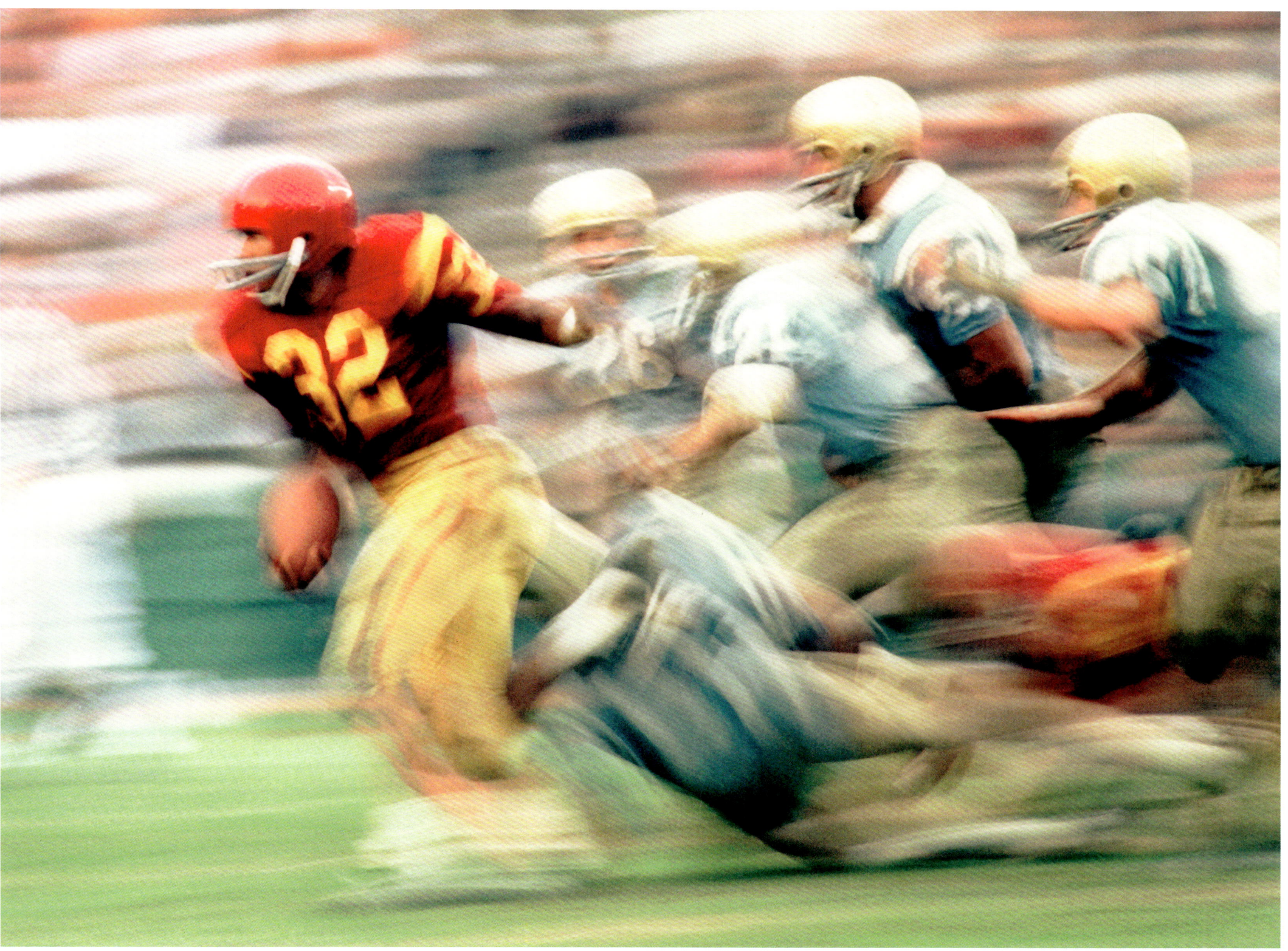

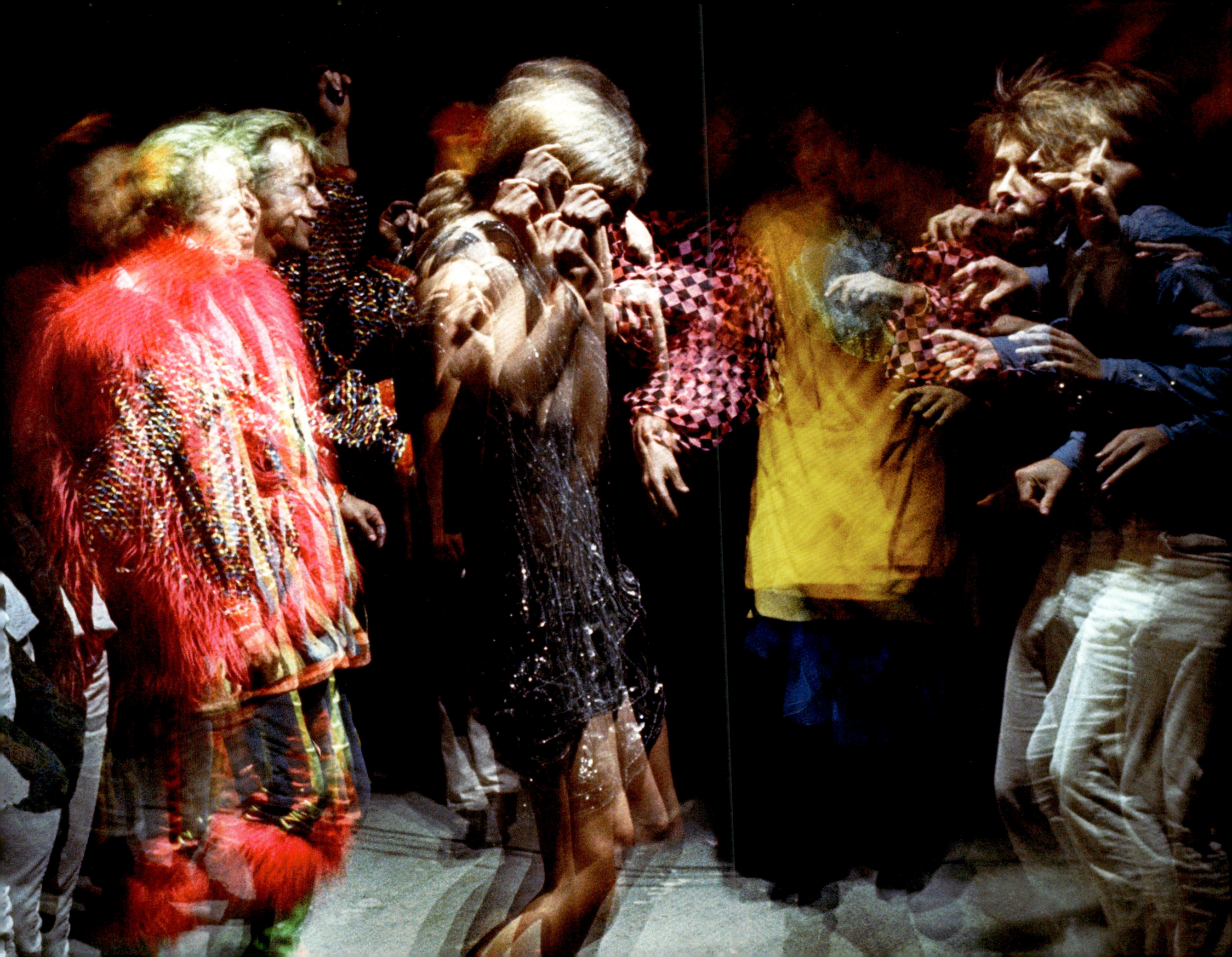

COUNTER CULTURE

Dennis Hopper was holed up in Taos, New Mexico, in 1971, submerging himself in the myth of his character from *Easy Rider*, when L.M.Kit Carson and I dropped in on him and began shooting our feature-length documentary, *The American Dreamer*. It soon became apparent to me that it was impossible to make a true documentary on Hopper; he was always performing for our cameras, playing an actor having a documentary made about him, blurring fact and fiction.

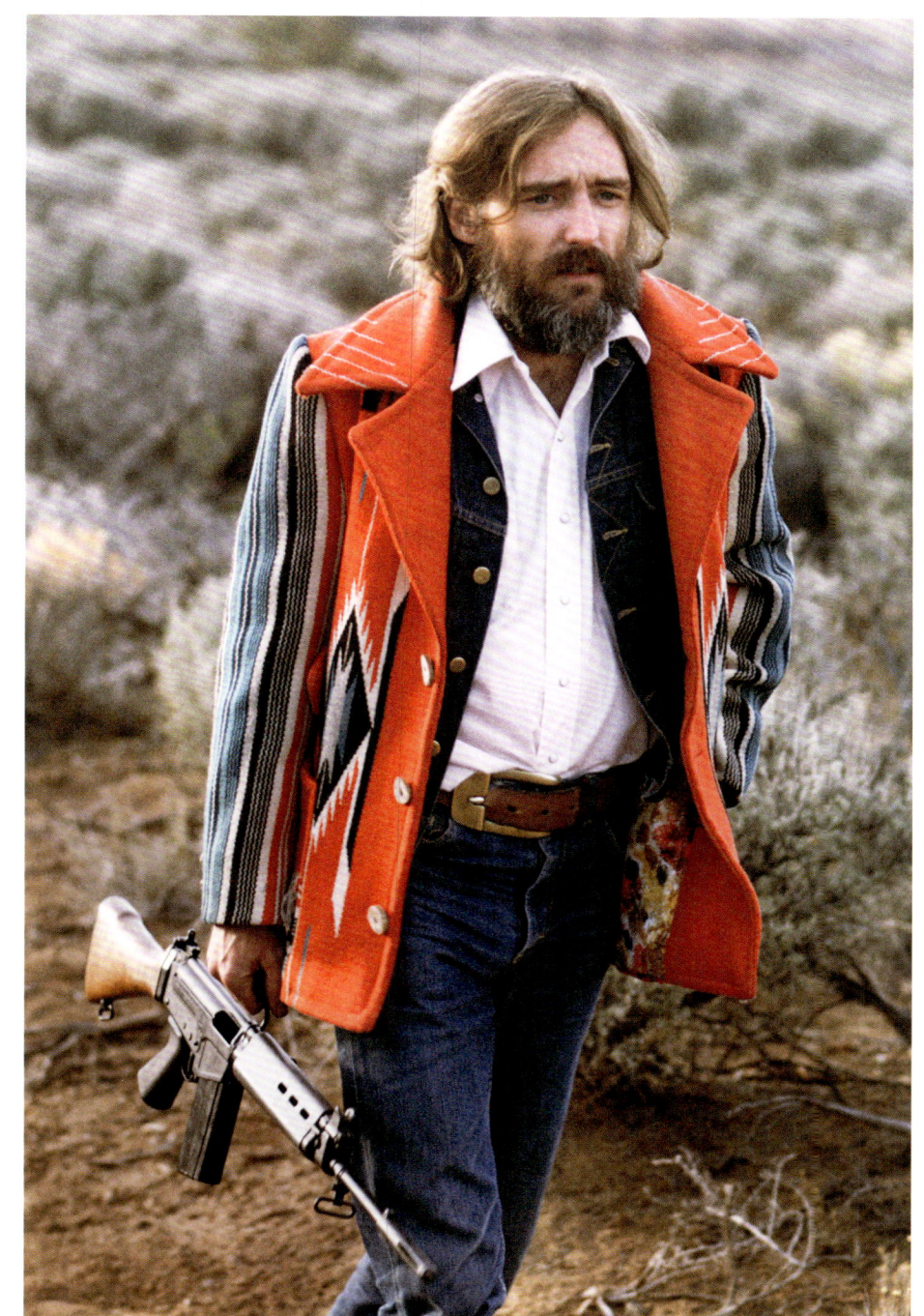

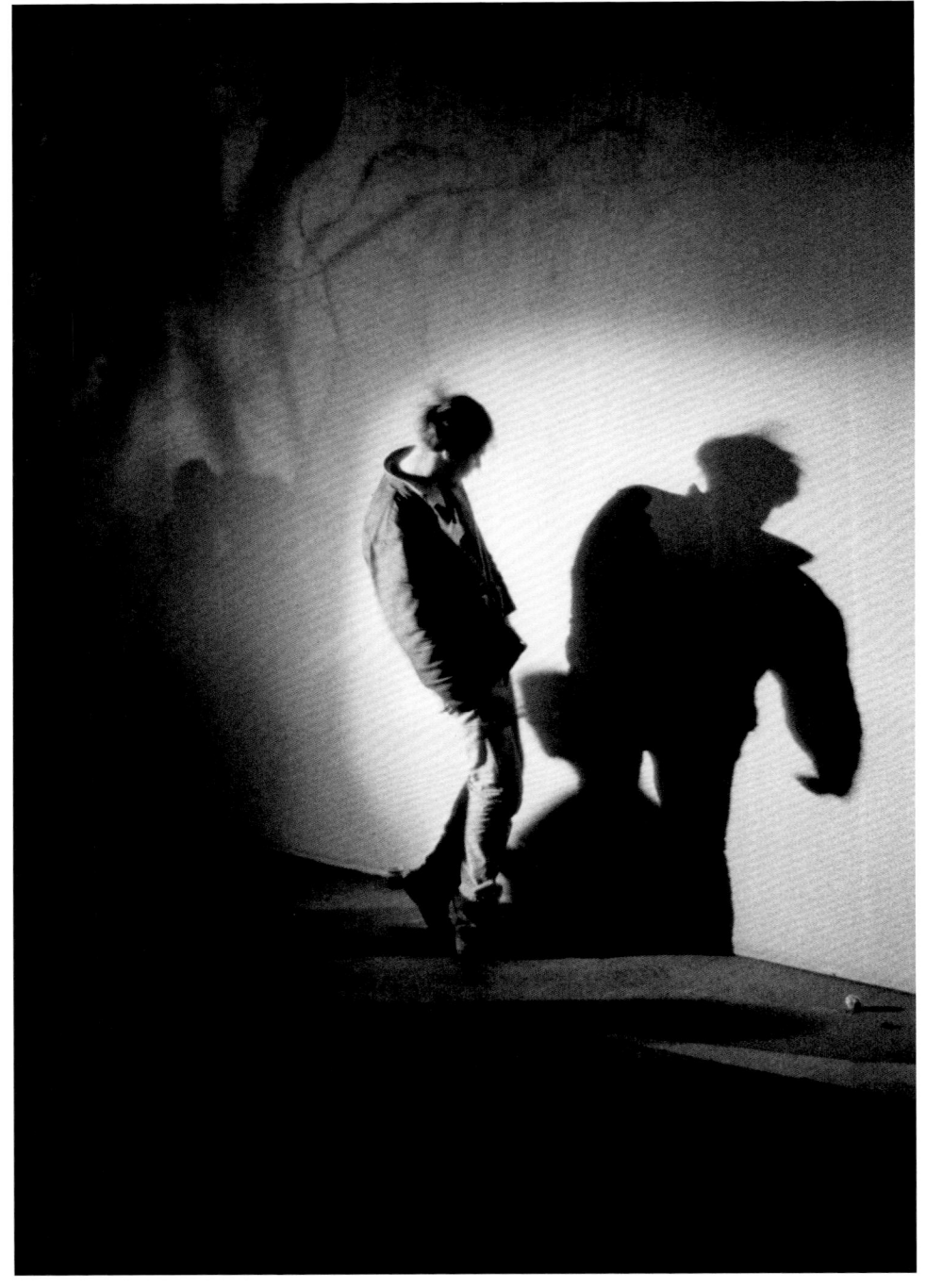
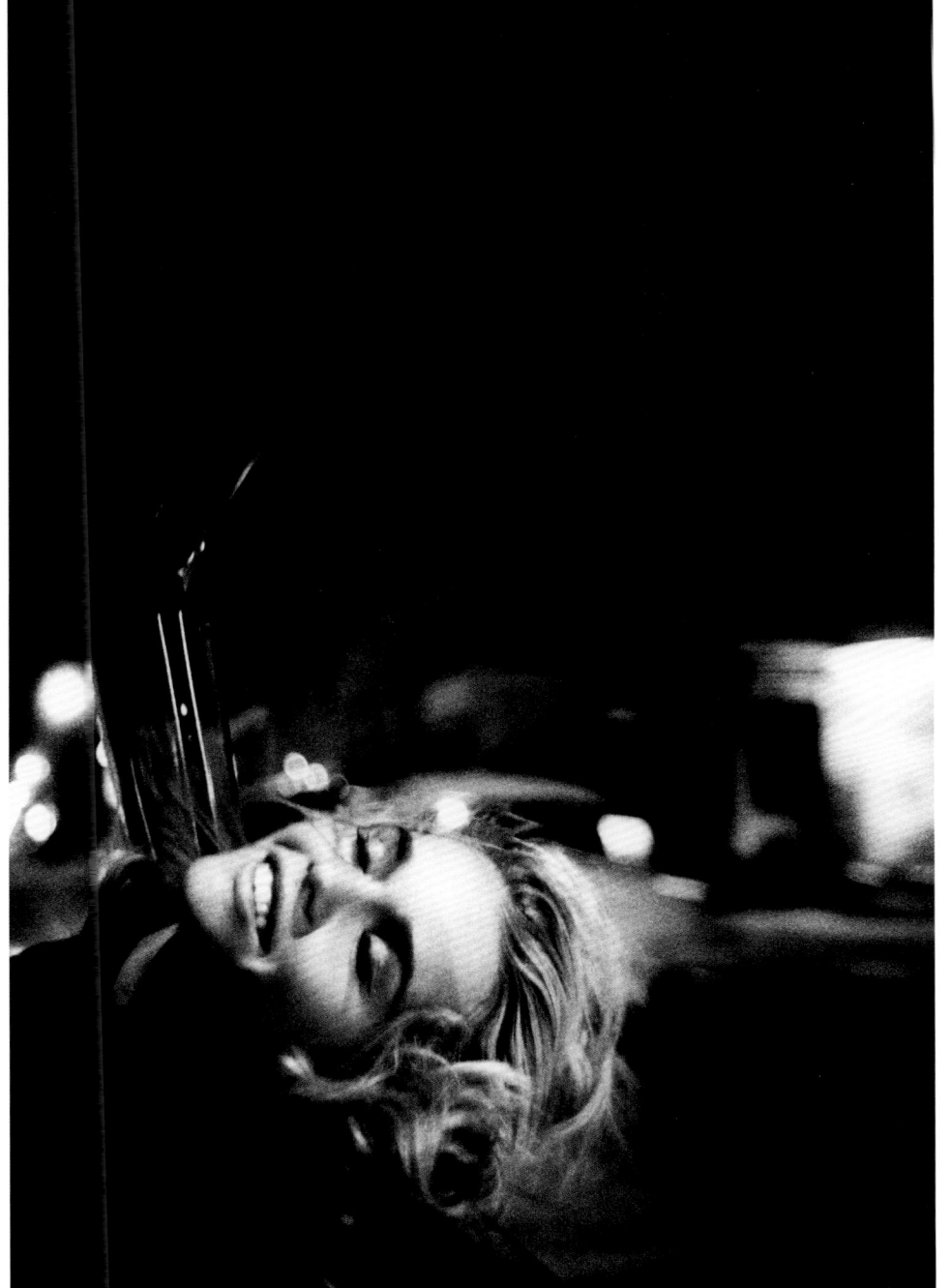

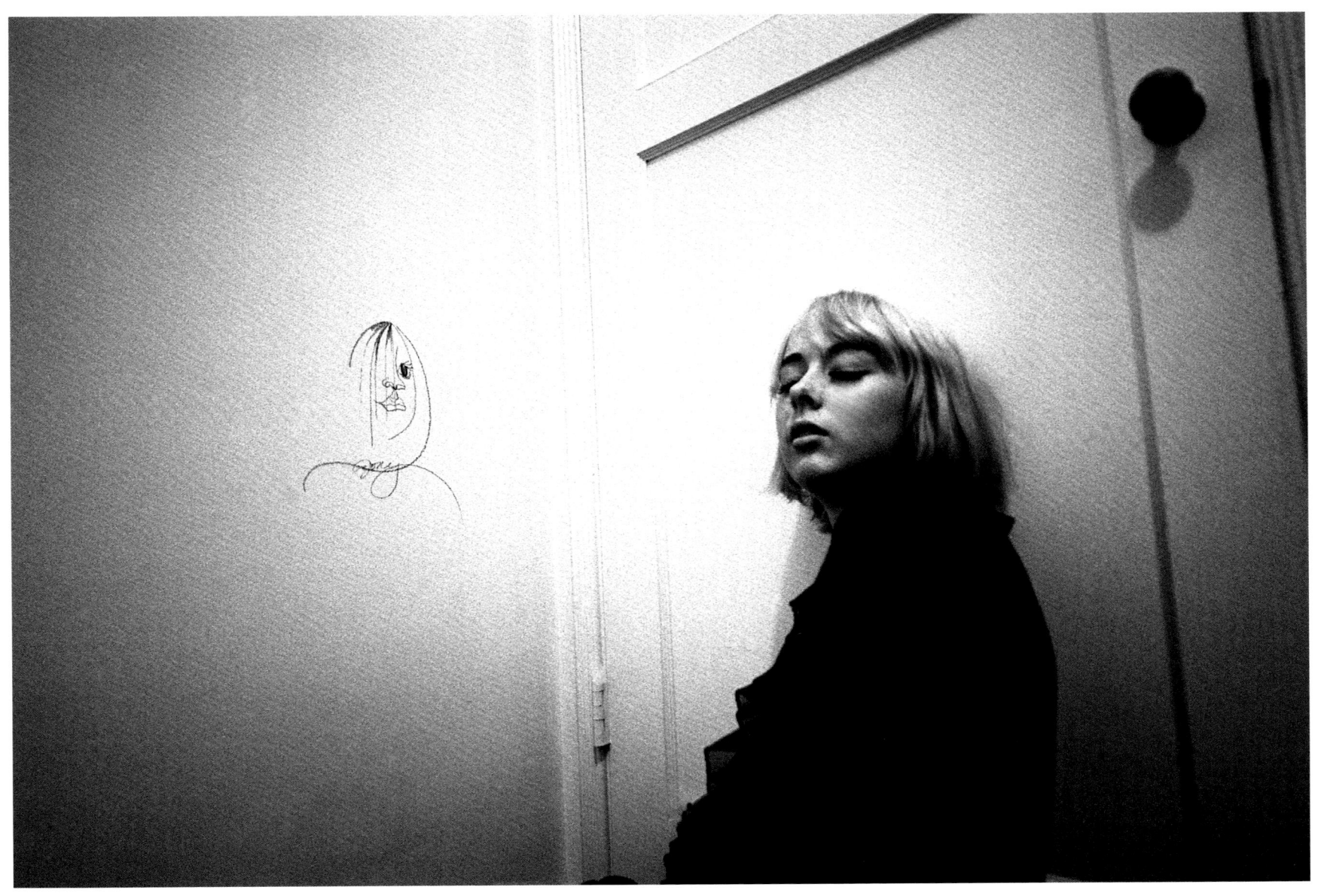

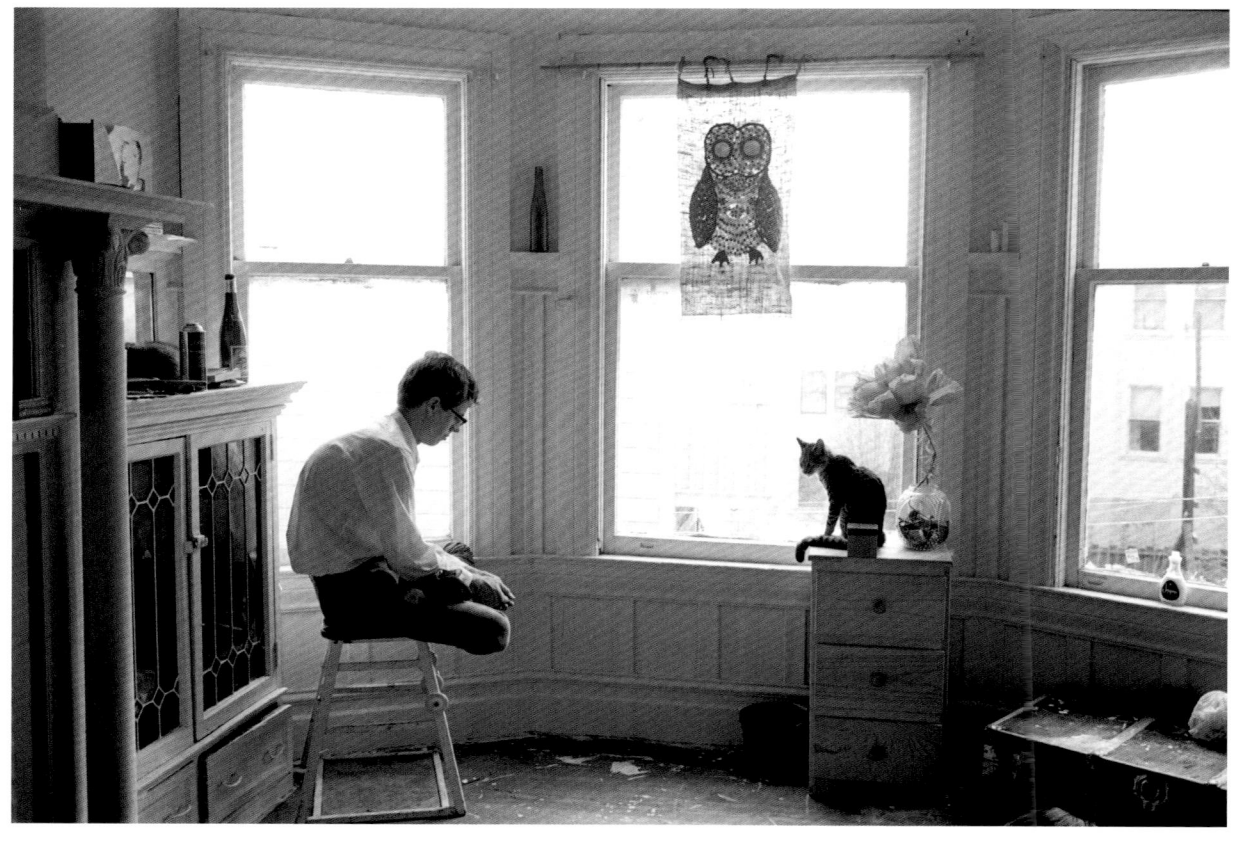

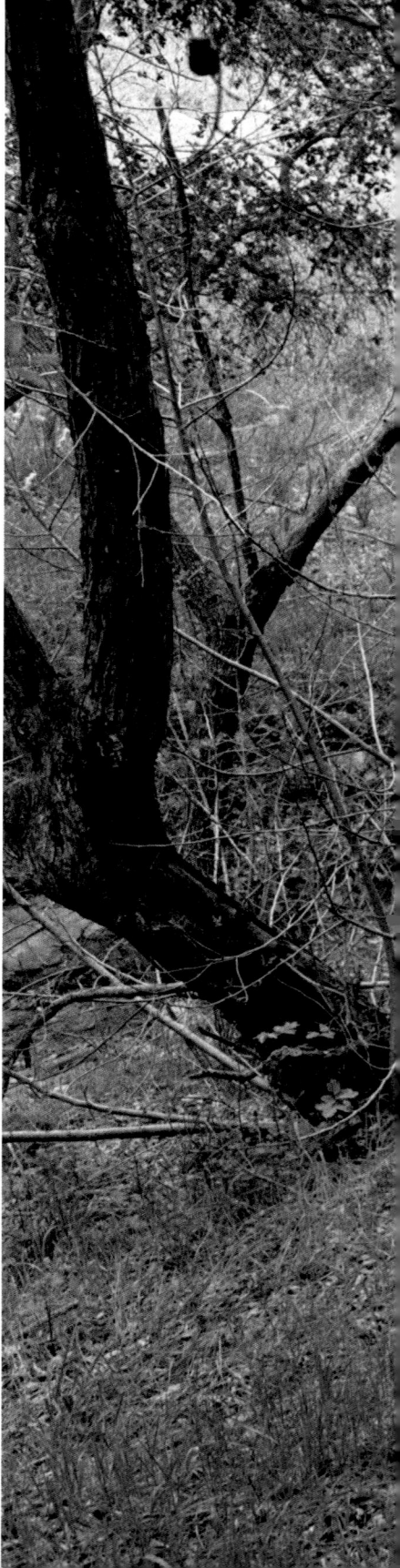

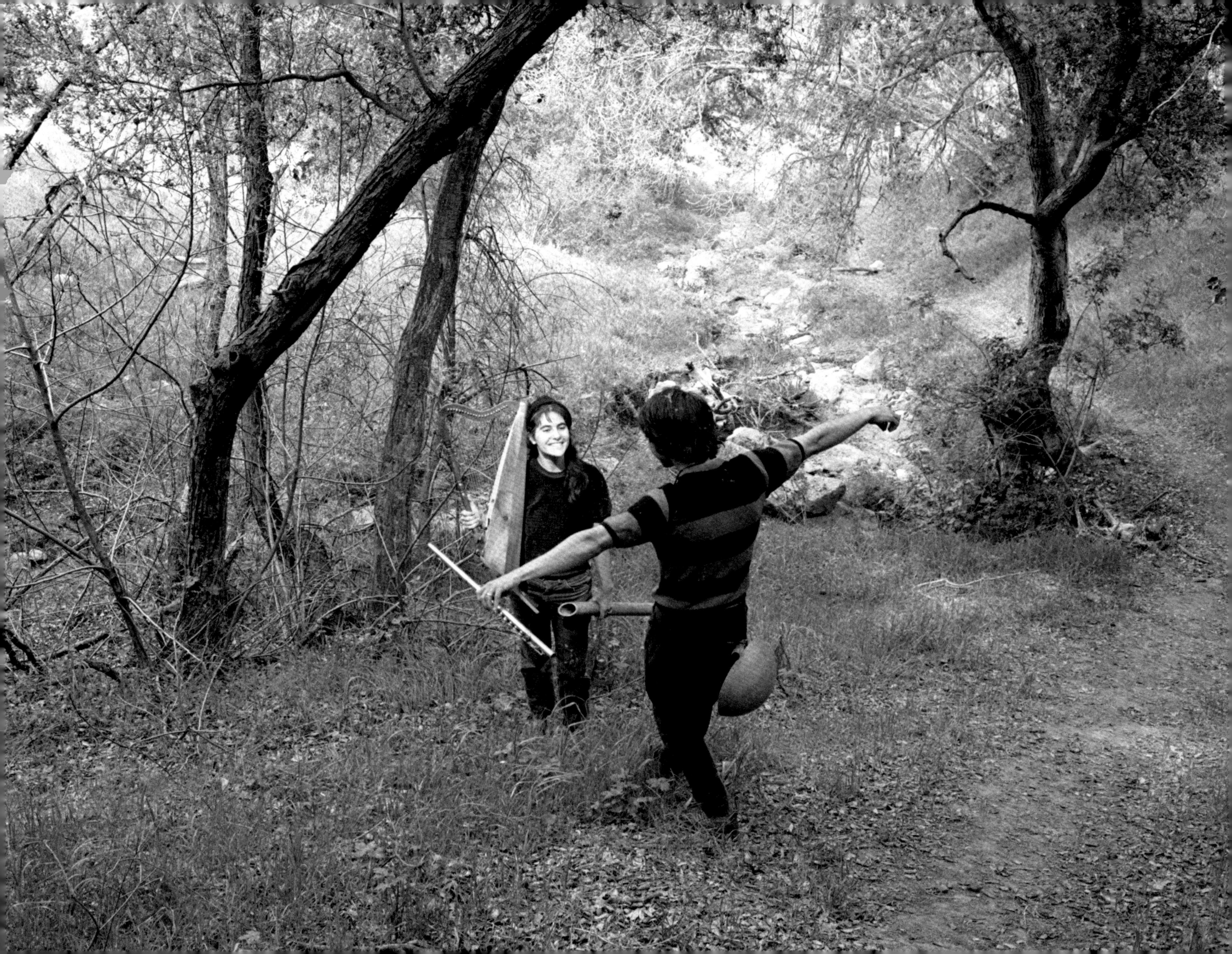

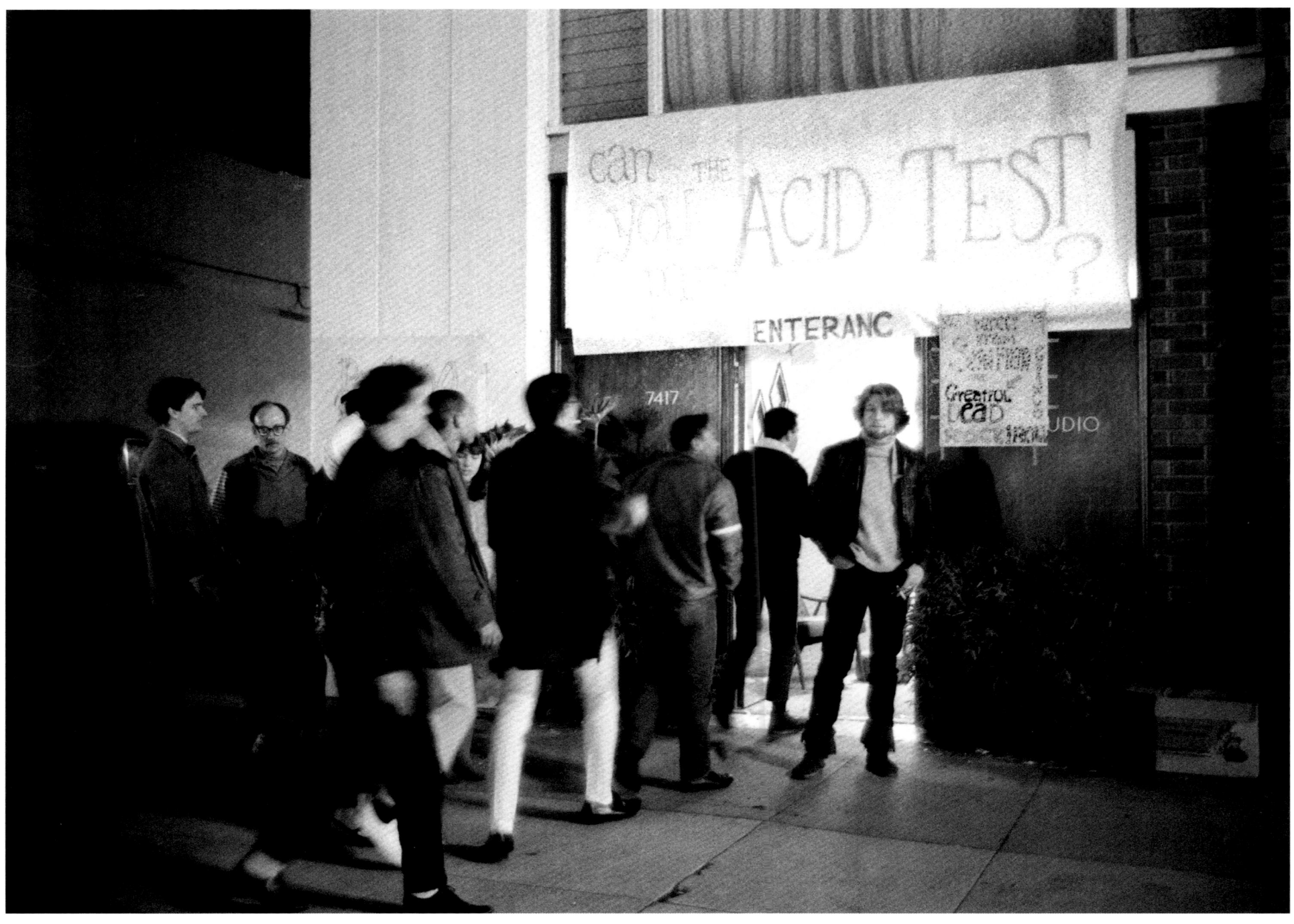

In 1966, I was the first to document the recreational use of LSD, from students in San Francisco to the acid scene at 3 a.m. near "Capsule Corner" in LA, right down the street from Canter's Delicatessen. Timothy Leary, Richard Alpert (later Ram Dass), Ken Kesey and his band of Merry Pranksters: I immersed myself in their world, and it wasn't long before I discovered that this story would soon become more than just a story; it would become part of my life and take on a life of its own.

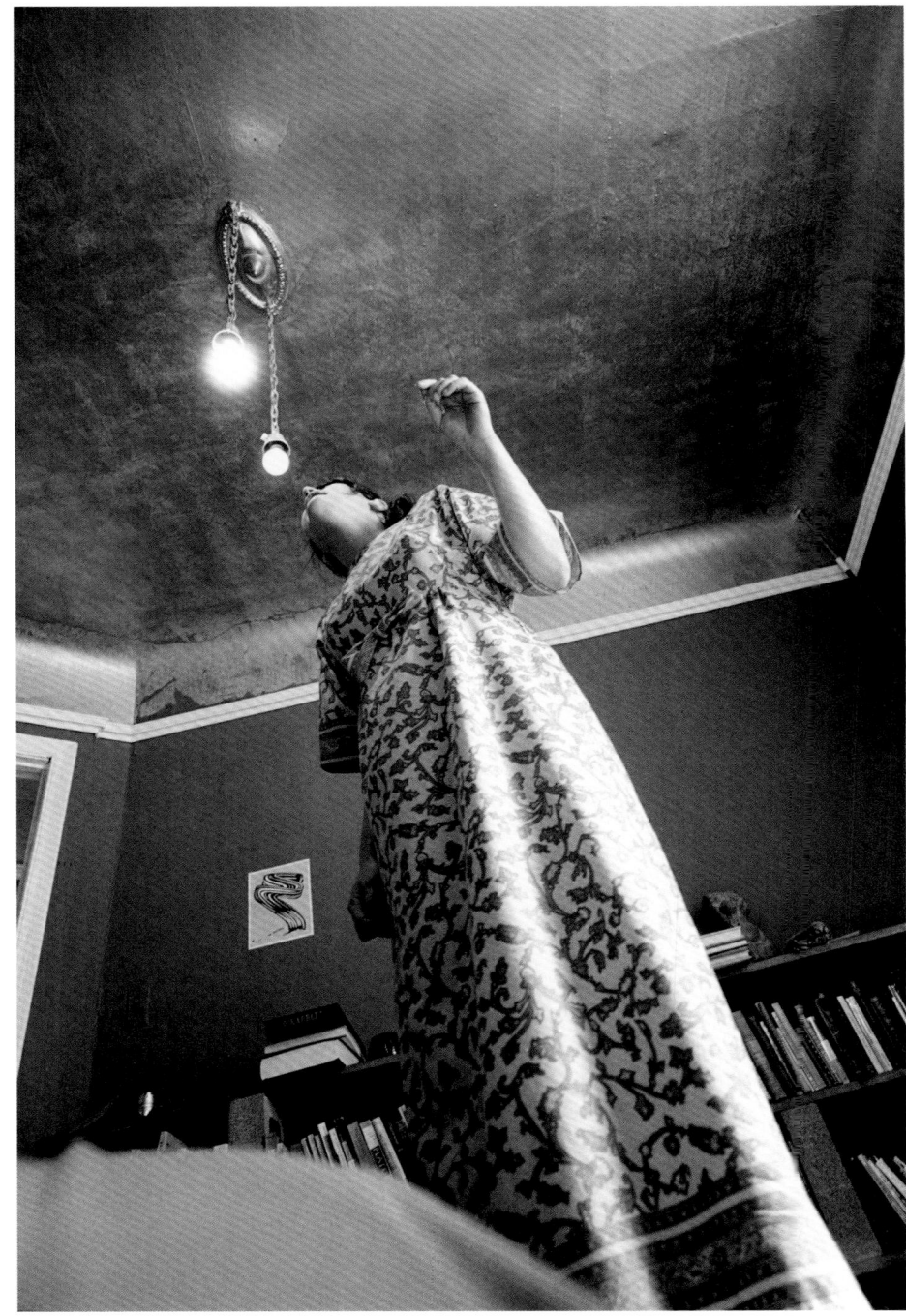

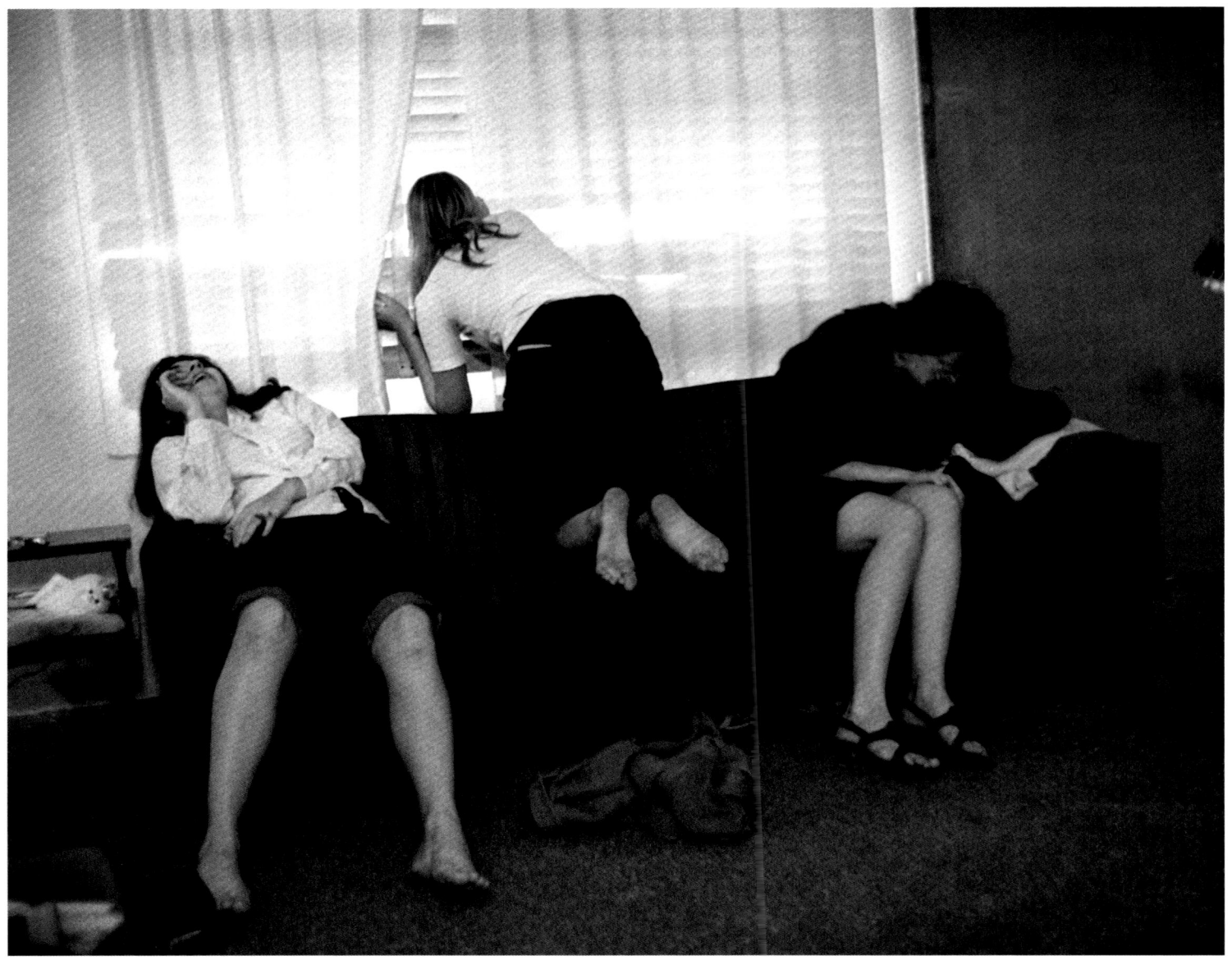

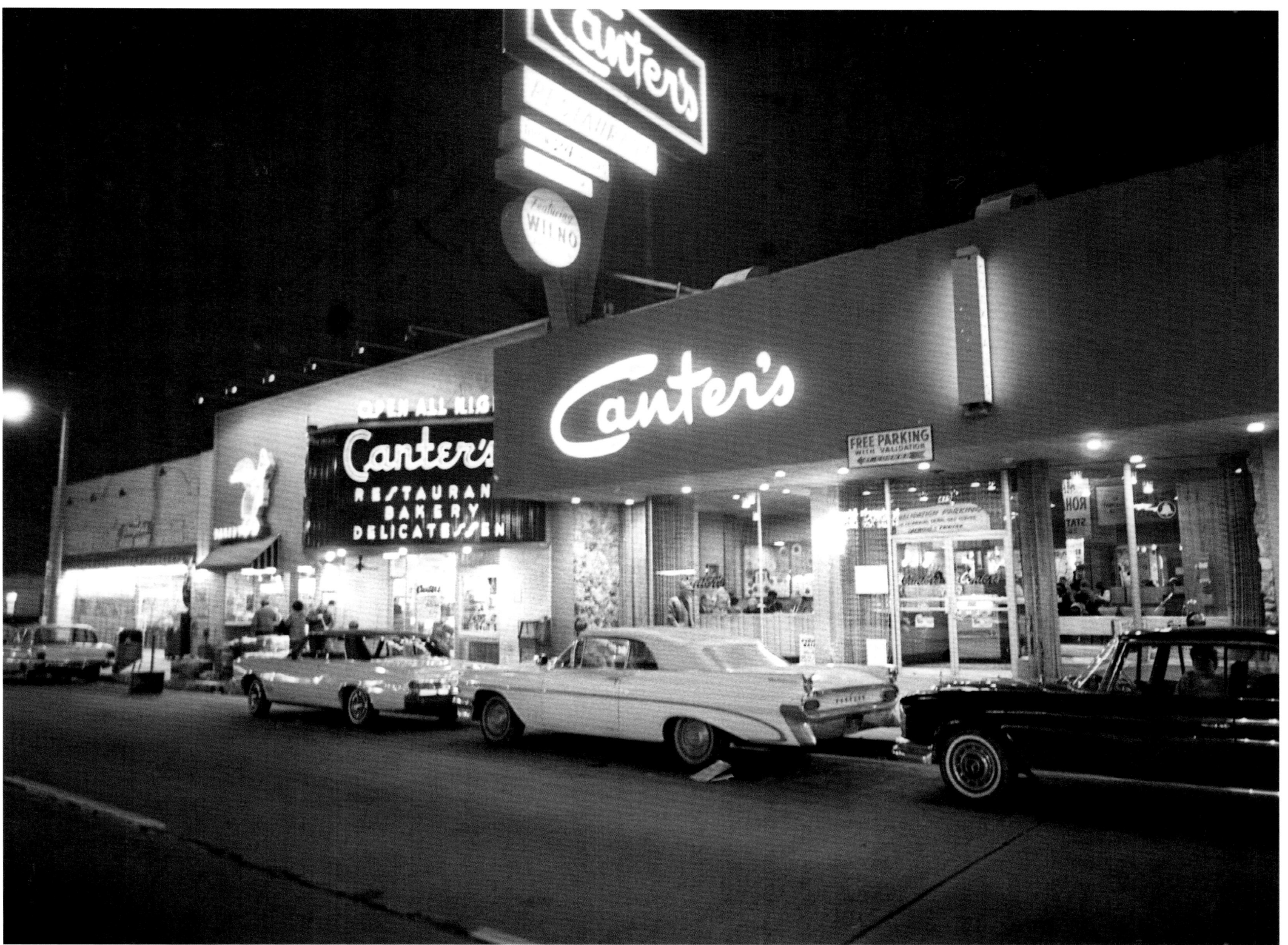

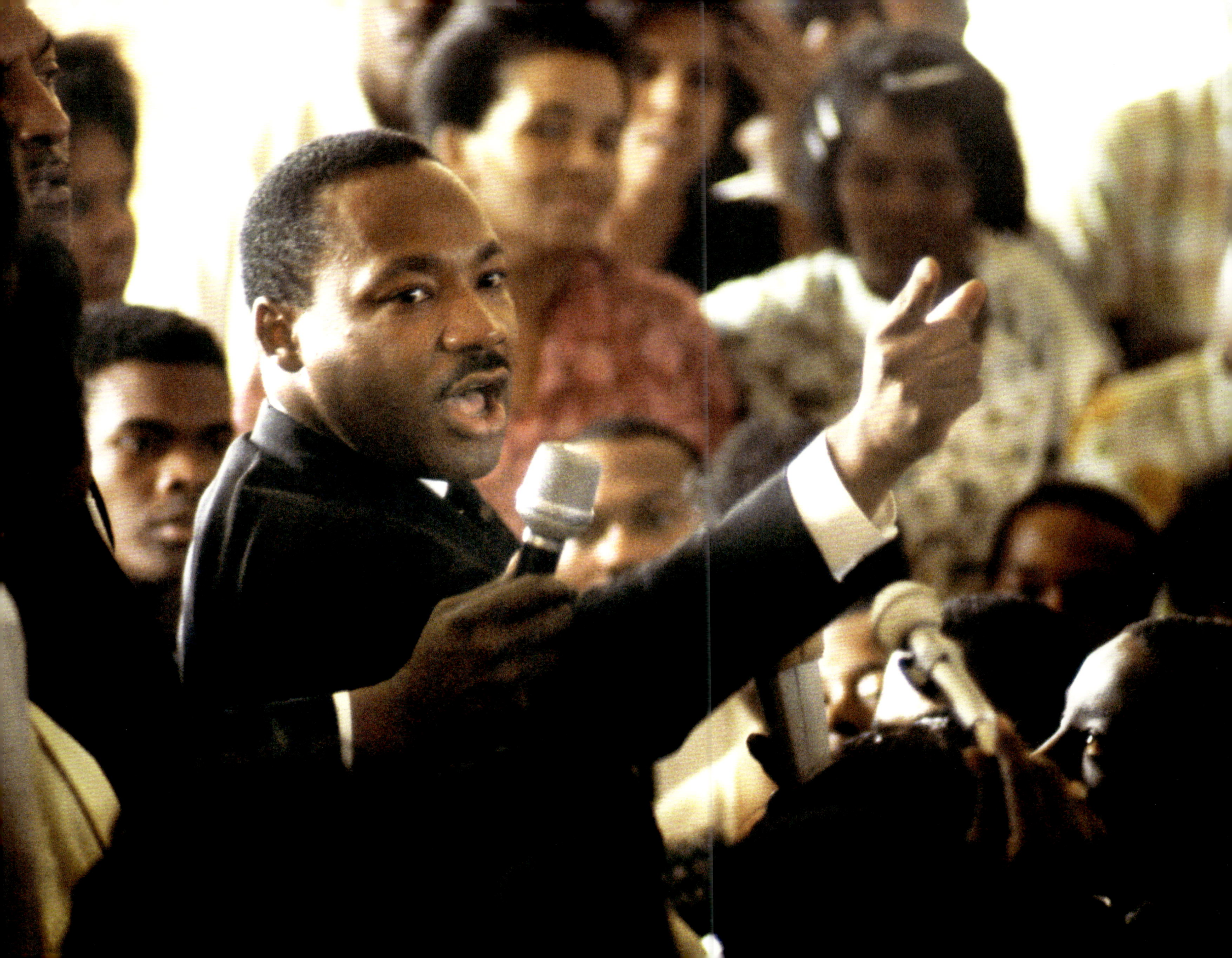

FALLEN HEROES

Not since the days of Lincoln had America been so at war with itself as it was in the Sixties — changes in our culture faced violent resistance during the most turbulent decade of my lifetime. The assassination of John F. Kennedy was not the first of the era, but for me it cast the longest shadow, and it haunts the pictures I later took of Dr. Martin Luther King, Jr., and Bobby Kennedy.

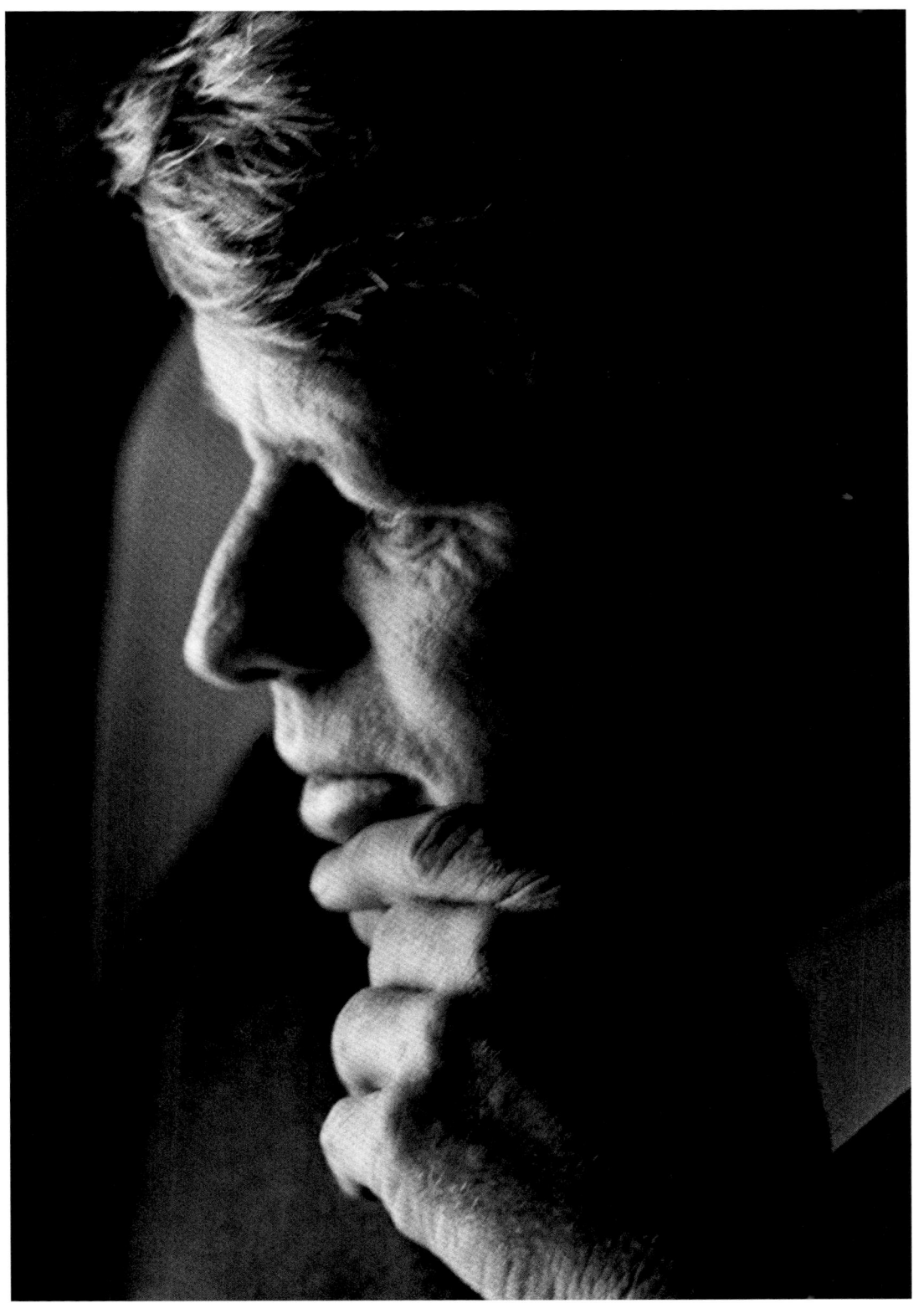

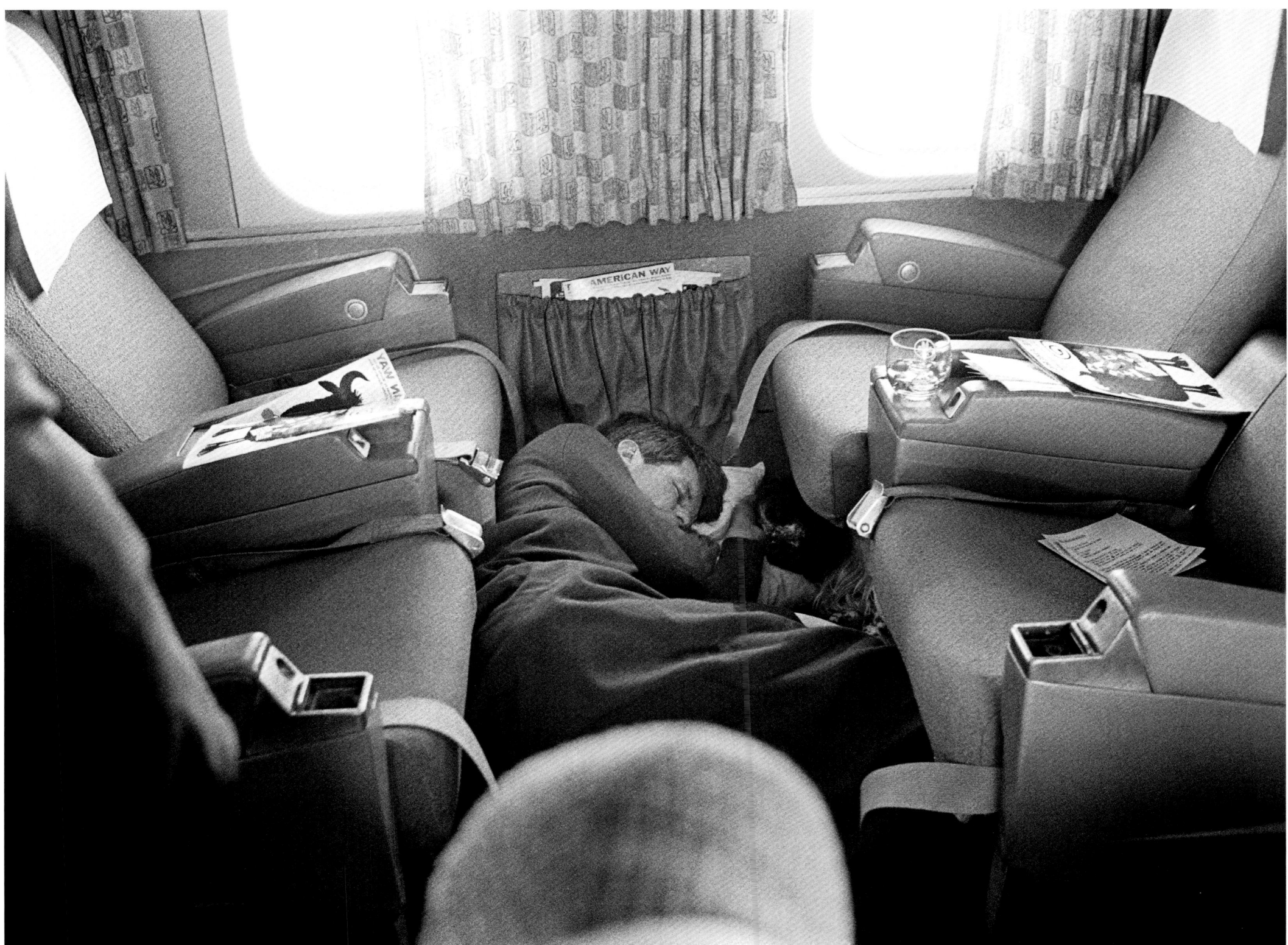

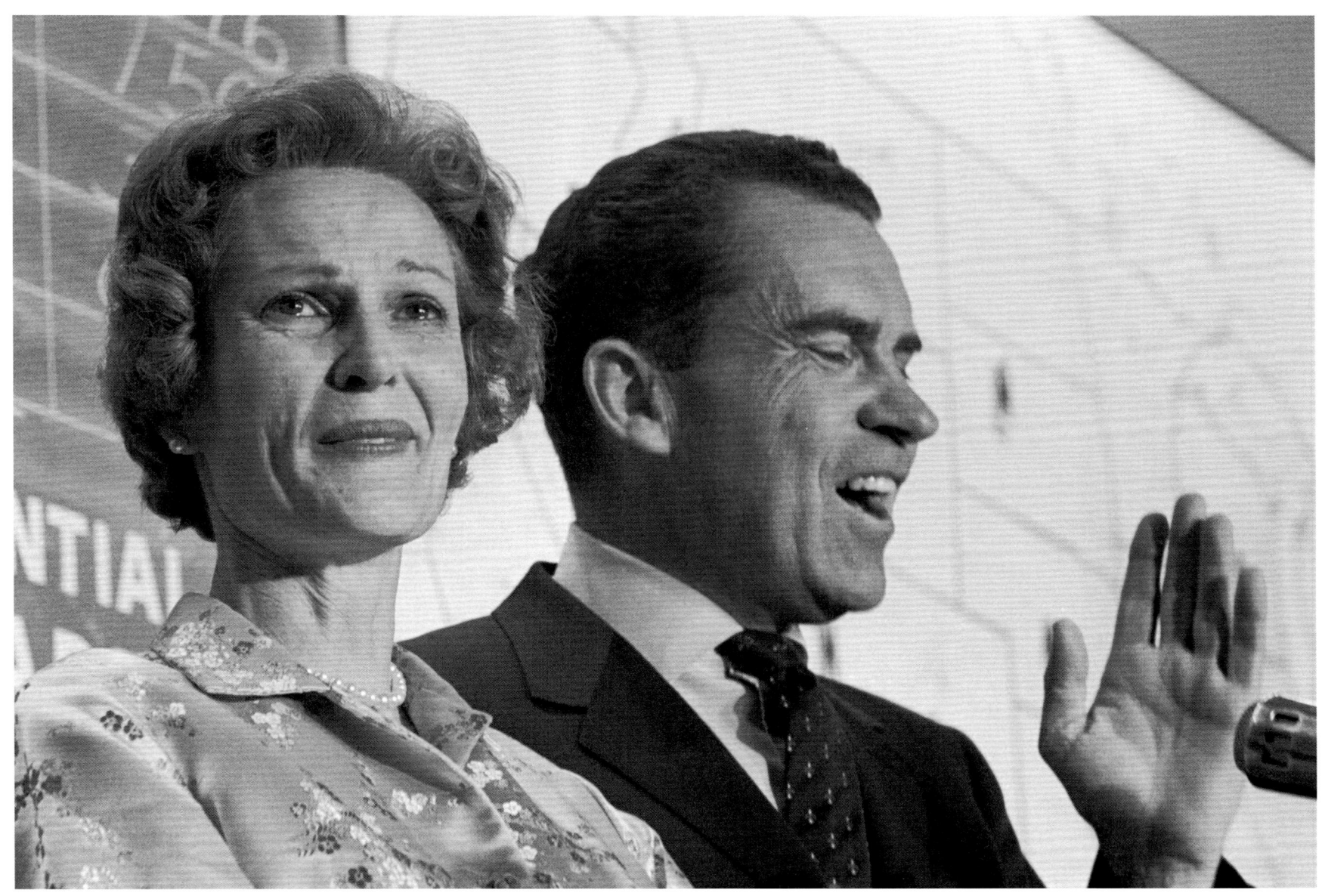

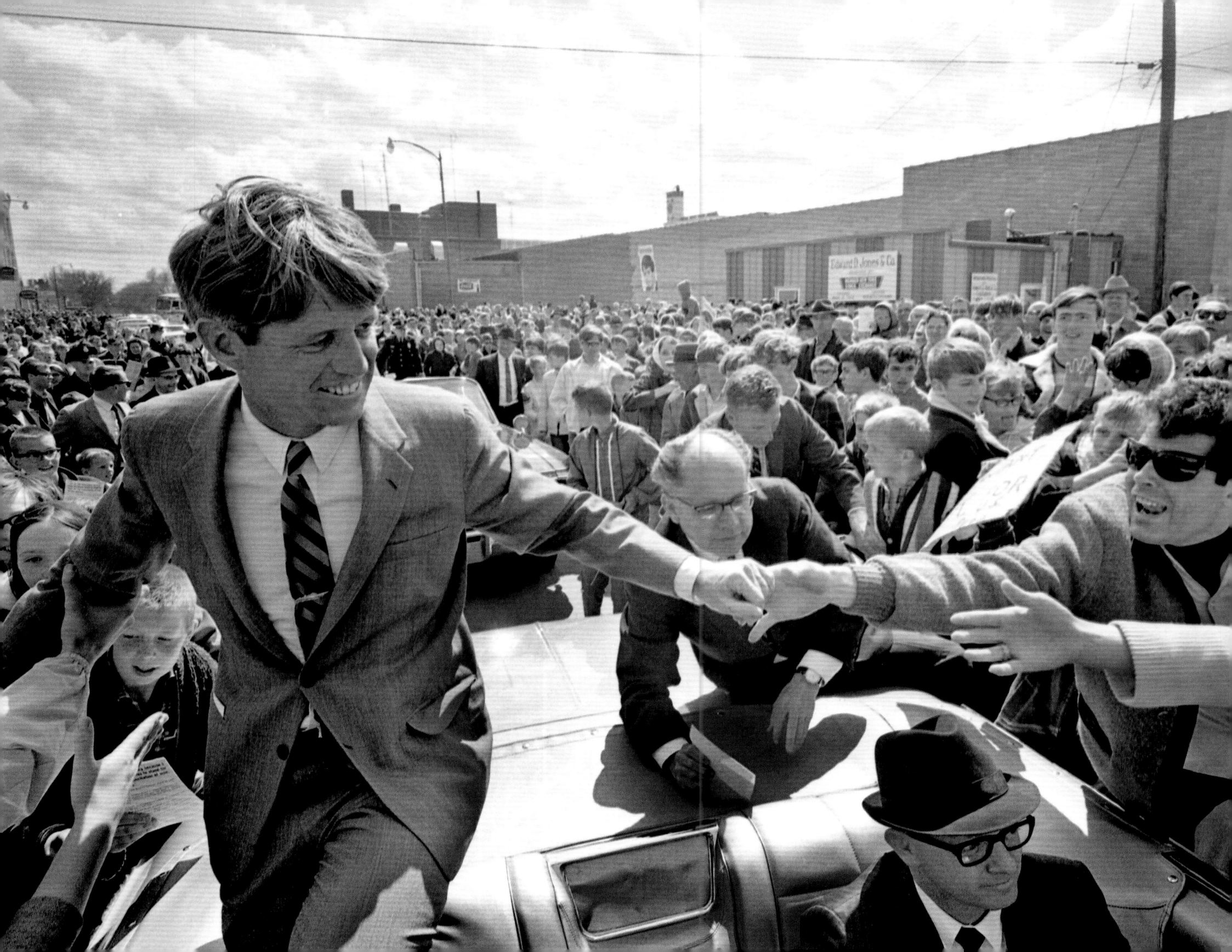

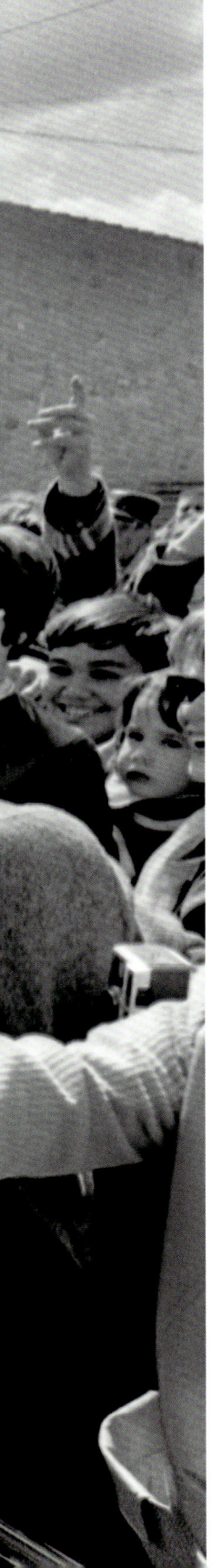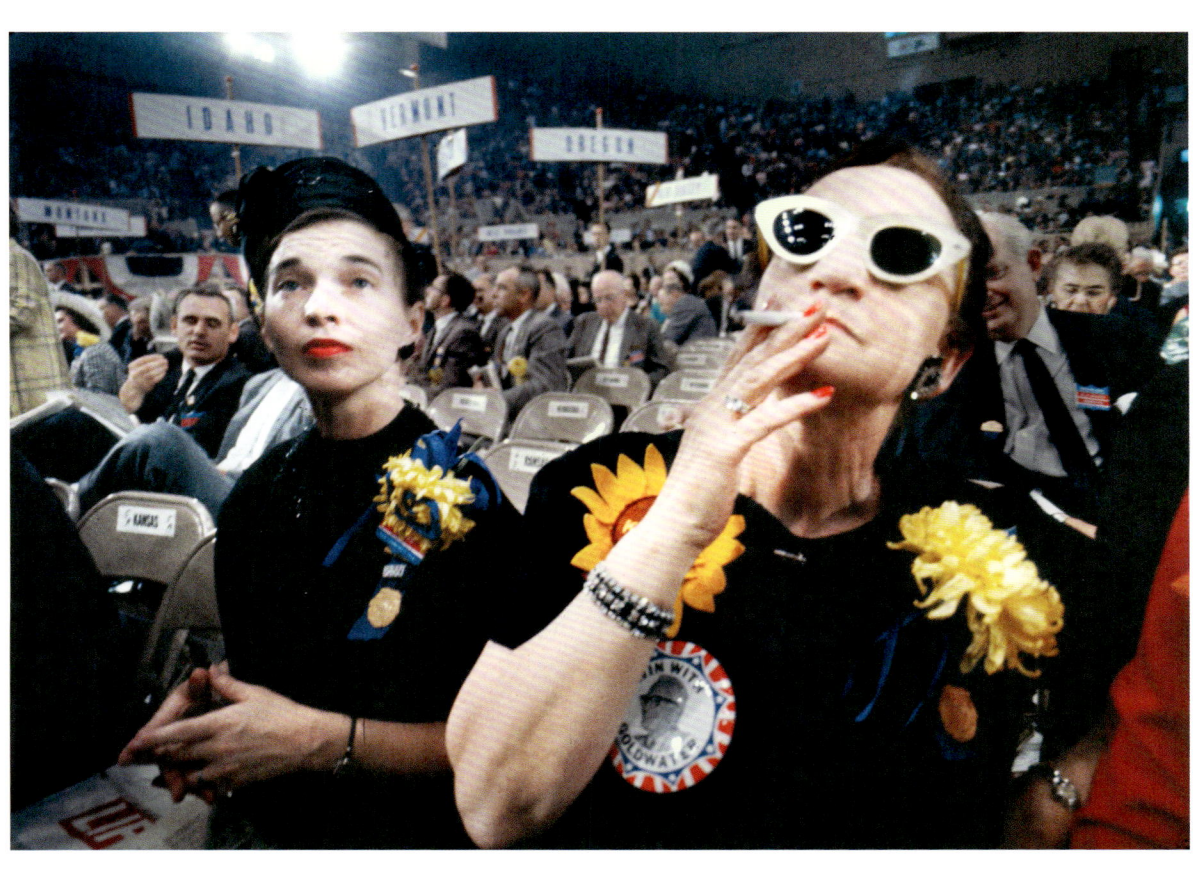

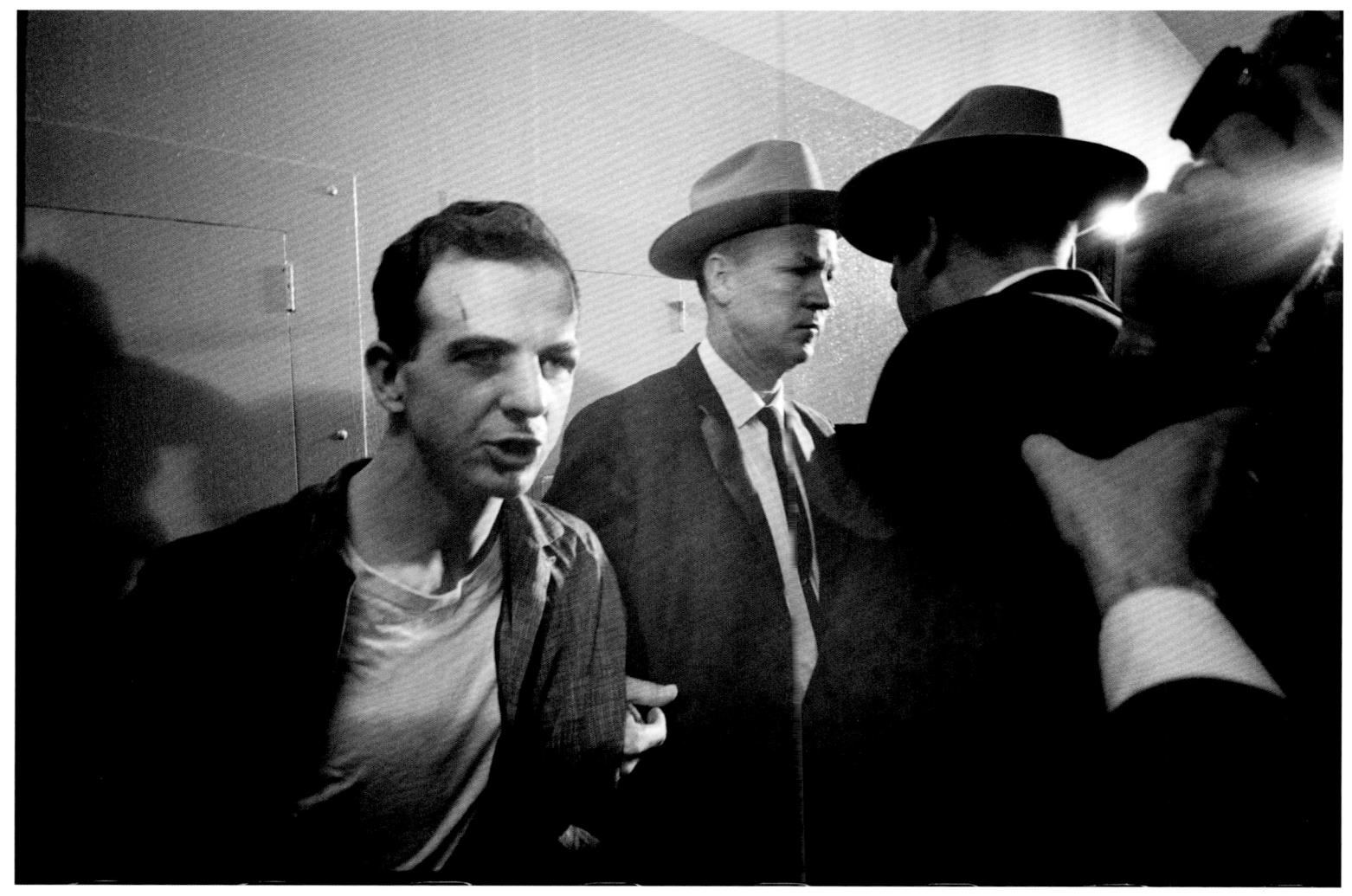

A few hours after President Kennedy was shot, I arrived at the Dallas Police Headquarters in time to witness Lee Harvey Oswald emerging from the elevator, handcuffed and surrounded by Texas Marshals. At that moment, what surprised me the most was that the man accused of killing Kennedy was practically the same age as me.

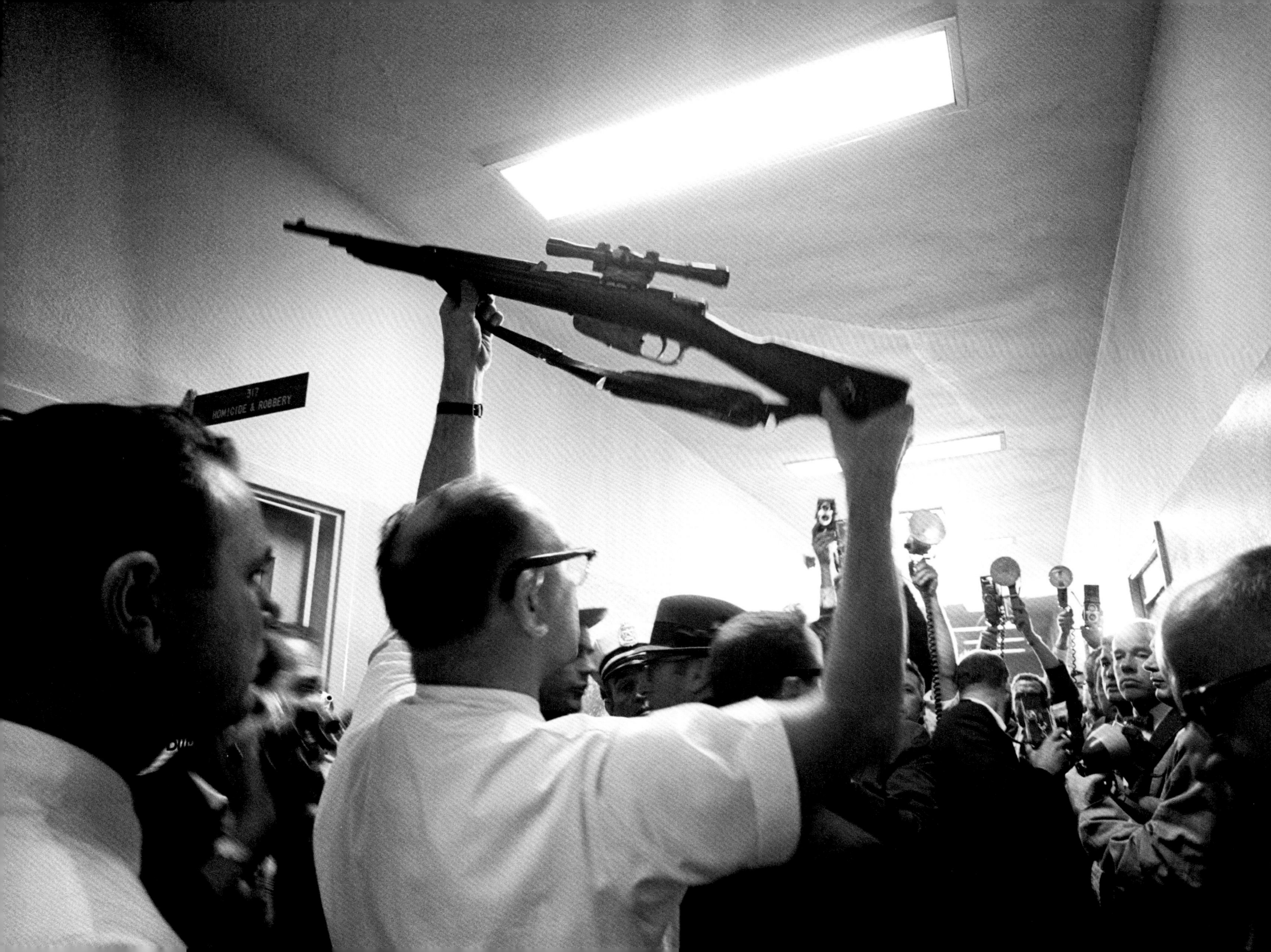

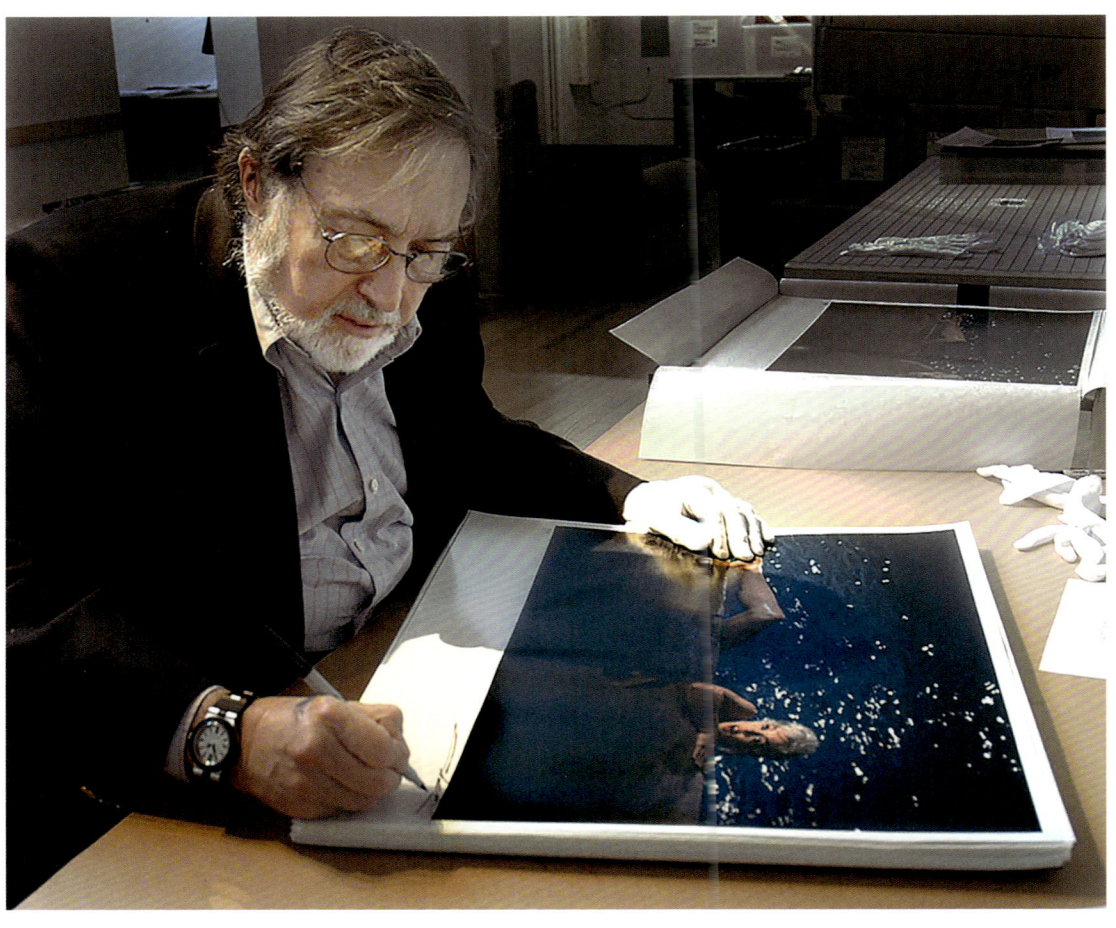

Lawrence Schiller is an American photojournalist, film producer, director, and author. His work has been featured in prominent magazines throughout the world. Schiller also directed a number of award-winning motion pictures, notably *The American Dreamer*, with Dennis Hopper, and *The Executioner's Song*, with Tommy Lee Jones. Schiller provided additional direction for *The Man Who Skied Down Everest* (1972), which won an Oscar for Best Documentary Feature.

Schiller has produced many books, his most notable being with his friend and colleague Norman Mailer. Over several decades, the two published *Marilyn* (1973), *The Faith of Graffiti* (1974), *Oswald's Tale* (1995), *Into the Mirror* (2002), and *The Executioner's Song* (1979), for which Mailer won the Pulitzer Prize. He is the author of the *New York Times* number-one best-selling *American Tragedy,* with James Willwerth (1996), *Barbra*, with Steve Schapiro (2016) and *Marilyn & Me* (2021). Schiller has consulted for NBC News, the John F. Kennedy Library Foundation, the Ray Bradbury estate, and the Annie Leibovitz Studio. After the death of Norman Mailer, Schiller was named the president and co-founder of the Norman Mailer Center and Writer's Colony in Provincetown, Massachusetts.

In 2023, Schiller's archives were transferred to the Dolph Briscoe Center for American History at the University of Texas in Austin, Texas. He is married to Nina Wiener and resides in Los Angeles.

Catalog design by Howard Schiller

Printed in Italy by Graphicom SpA, 2024

ISBN Hardcover: 979-8-9871128-1-6
ISBN Softcover: 979-8-9871128-2-3
Library of Congress Control Number: 2024913242

Published by WS Press, Los Angeles

For special sales and bulk orders,
please contact wspi.353@gmail.com.

lawrenceschiller.com